THE BOOK OF
BISCUITS

PAT ALBUREY

Photography by
JON STEWART

Published by Salamander Books Limited
LONDON • NEW YORK

Published 1988 by Salamander Books Ltd,
52 Bedford Row, London WC1R 4LR
By arrangement with Merehurst Press,
5 Great James Street, London WC1N 3DA

ISBN: 0 86101 282 8

Managing Editor: Felicity Jackson
Editor: Louise Steele
Designer: Roger Daniels
Home Economist: Pat Alburey
Photographer: Jon Stewart, assisted by Alister Thorpe
Typeset by Angel Graphics
Colour separation by J. Film Process Ltd, Bangkok, Thailand.
Printed in Belgium by Proost International Book Production

ACKNOWLEDGEMENTS

The publishers would like to thank the following for their
help and advice:
China supplied by Chinacraft of London, 499 Oxford Street,
London W1 and branches
Lawleys, 154 Regent Street, London W1
Philips Home Appliances   City House, 420-430 London
Road, Croydon CR9 3QR

Companion volumes of interest:
The Book of COCKTAILS
The Book of CHOCOLATES & PETITS FOURS
The Book of HORS D'OEUVRES
The Book of GARNISHES
The Book of PRESERVES
The Book of SAUCES
The Book of ICE CREAMS & SORBETS
The Book of GIFTS FROM THE PANTRY
The Book of PASTA
The Book of HOT & SPICY NIBBLES – DIPS – DISHES
The Book of CRÊPES & OMELETTES
The Book of FONDUES
The Book of CHEESECAKES

CONTENTS

INTRODUCTION

Biscuit, or cookie, is the name given to an infinite number of small plain, sweet, or semi-sweet confections that have, over the years, become great favourites the world over, with adults and children alike. Savoury biscuits are equally as popular, and are mainly referred to as crackers. In fact, the earliest biscuits were not sweet: they were simply hard flat rounds of unleavened flour and water paste. However, from their humble beginnings, biscuits have developed through the centuries into the irresistible delicacies we know today, with famous classics like gingerbread, florentines, macaroons, brandy snaps and shortbread being produced along the way.

The Book of Biscuits contains recipes for them all, plus a host of others ranging from simple oatcakes to a magnificent gingerbread house. There are over 100 recipes (all with helpful step-by-step photographs), and something to suit all tastes – homely, chunky biscuits; plain and rich ones; those that are crisp, light and delicate; savoury and wholefood biscuits and special ones for the festive times of the year. There is even a selection of delicious no-bake biscuits.

You do not have to be an experienced cook to be able to make successful biscuits for they are exceptionally easy to prepare, requiring surprisingly little, or no, special equipment. And most are simple enough for children to make. Home-made biscuits, as well as being delicious, are also economical and you will be surprised at the large number of biscuits that can be made from relatively few ingredients.

The aroma of freshly-baked biscuits is as much to be enjoyed as is the pleasure of making and eating them. If you have not already discovered the joys of biscuit making, then beware, this book can become addictive!

EQUIPMENT

The delightful thing about biscuit making is that it requires the minimum of essential equipment — namely, a mixing bowl, measuring scales, measuring spoons, a rolling pin (though in some cases even this is not required), a knife, baking sheet and wire rack. With just these few things you will be able to make a vast number of different biscuits. However, if you would like to widen your repertoire it is worthwhile investing in some additional equipment. Buy the extra things gradually, as your skill and enthusiasm grows.

For Making
As for all baking, accurate measuring is most important. Use proper measuring spoons (instead of ordinary household spoons). These are inexpensive to buy and widely available. A good set of scales, preferably balance scales, or standard measuring cups are also essential, and for fluid measurements you will need an accurate measuring jug. A large sieve is necessary for the even blending of flour with raising agents and spices.

Rolling Out
The rolling pin you use should be fairly long with smooth rounded ends (fancy handles and knobbed ends mark the dough). However, there are ridged rolling pins made specifically for the purpose of marking rolled-out dough.

Any smooth work surface, or large wooden pastry board can be used for rolling out biscuit doughs. Although not essential, a large marble slab is an asset, particularly for the richer softer doughs (as it keeps beautifully cool).

Shaping
Simple shapes such as squares, oblongs, triangles and diamonds can be cut by hand with a knife. For this a thin-bladed knife is best, especially for cutting through refrigerated biscuit doughs. A pastry wheel gives a decorative edge to simple shapes.

Cutters can be bought in all shapes and sizes, from plain rounds to fancy shapes, figures, animal shapes, letters and numerals. When buying shaped cutters, make sure that they have a good cutting edge, to cut through the dough cleanly and give a well defined outline. Metal cutters are usually best, as unfortunately plastic ones do not always cut well. Sets of shaped cutters, contained in a tin, are a very good buy as they give a range of sizes. All the cutter measurements in recipes were taken across the cutting edge (most

cutters have a rolled top edge which give a different measurement). The measurements are given as a guide, but you can, of course, choose sizes and shapes to suit yourself.

For quick cutting out, cutters contained on a biscuit roller are very useful as all you have to do is roll them across the rolled-out dough.

Many biscuit doughs, and meringue based biscuits, are formed into shape with a piping bag and nozzle. Choose a bag with a welded seam in preference to a stitched seam – these are stronger and there are no holes for the mixture to ooze out through. Metal nozzles give a more defined shape than plastic ones.

A mechanical biscuit press is a must for the enthusiast. They come complete with an assortment of discs to produce very professional looking fancy shapes, and enable a vast number of biscuits to be quickly made.

A luxury item is a shortbread mould. They are fairly expensive and are really only worthwhile buying if you make a lot of shortbread–particularly for gifts.

For no-bake, bar and slab biscuits, a shallow baking tin or Swiss roll tin is essential. Heavy guage Swiss roll tins can also be used as baking sheets. Beware of some of the thinner metal tins as they can buckle in the oven.

Baking and Cooling

Baking sheets should be of a heavy guage metal to ensure that they do not buckle in the oven. Buy the largest size your oven will take, to enable you to bake as many biscuits as possible in one go (unless the recipe states otherwise).

Non-stick baking paper is the perfect answer to prevent rich doughs and meringues sticking to baking sheets.

A flexible palette knife is useful for removing biscuits from baking sheets and one or two wire racks are essential for cooling biscuits.

Finishing

A pastry brush is necessary for brushing biscuits with glazes, both before and after baking, and for removing excess flour from surface of rolled-out doughs.

Storing

Store biscuits in an airtight container. Traditional biscuit tins are perfect and there are now very many attractively decorated ones from which to choose.

Care of equipment

Metal baking sheets and metal cutters become rusty if they are not dried well after washing. To prevent this happening, put them in a warm oven to dry before storing away.

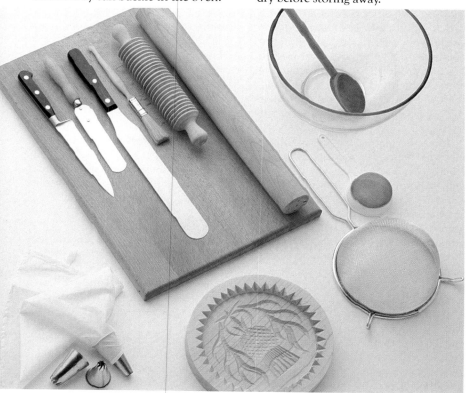

— BISCUIT MAKING METHODS —

Although biscuits come in an infinite variety of shapes, sizes, textures and flavours, the basic methods for making them are relatively few, and quite simple: following closely those used for pastry and cake making. They are as follows: the traditional rubbed-in; creamed; whisked and melting methods; plus a few unusual ones for biscuits that do not have to be baked, and for those that are meringue-based.

For the best flavour, use butter, unsalted or salted, with a good flavour. You can, of course, use margarine if you prefer but the flavour will not be as good.

Rubbed-in Method

This is used to make very plain to very rich biscuits. The dough is mainly rolled out, then cut into shapes. It can sometimes be rolled into shapes by hand. Butter is incorporated into the flour, by being rubbed-in with the fingertips, until the mixture resembles fine breadcrumbs. To prevent the dough becoming soft and sticky, particularly when using a very high proportion of butter to flour, use cold firm butter. Handle the dough lightly and as little as possible.

Plain and self-raising flours can both be used, as well as plain flour with the addition of baking powder to make a light crisp biscuit. The texture of the finished biscuit will vary according to the amount of butter and sugar used to the quantity of flour. The higher the butter content, the softer the biscuit; the lower the butter content and higher the sugar content, the crisper the biscuit.

After the butter has been rubbed into the flour, the mixture is bound together with whole egg, egg yolks, or milk to form a dough firm enough to roll out. Size 3 (60-65 g) eggs are used for the recipes in this book, unless otherwise stated. When a high proportion of butter is used, as for some shortbreads, no binding ingredient (such as egg or milk) is required.

Creamed Method

The creamed method produces a varying range of textures, from crisp and brittle, to the soft, melt-in-the-mouth varieties. The dough can be made firm enough to be rolled out with a rolling pin, or may be rolled into shape by hand. It may also be soft enough to be forced through a piping nozzle, or biscuit press: or very soft, to be dropped from a spoon onto the baking sheet.

The butter is beaten with sugar until it is very creamy in appearance and light and fluffy in texture.

Creaming can be done by hand with a wooden spoon, or using a hand-held electric mixer. Large quantities can be creamed in a large electric mixer.

As the flour added is proportionally very much higher than that added to cake mixtures, you will, after an initial blending in with a spoon, need to work the ingredients together by hand to form a dough. You could work the flour in completely by hand, but this can make the dough soft and sticky.

Creamed doughs will be softer than those made by the rubbed-in method. Most can be kneaded and rolled out immediately, but some do need to be chilled until firm enough to roll out. Where this is absolutely necessary, refrigeration is recommended in the recipe. If it is not specifically mentioned, and you do not feel confident enough to handle a softer dough, simply wrap it in plastic wrap and refrigerate it for a short while until firm. However, do not allow the dough to become too hard as this makes it difficult to roll out and causes it to crack.

Always refrigerate a dough rather than be tempted to knead in extra flour, as this changes the texture of the biscuit. Also, remember that when the trimmings are re-kneaded and re-rolled, the dough becomes drier as it takes in extra flour. Mixtures with a high proportion of sugar are softer than those with a lower amount and these benefit by being chilled both before rolling out, and before baking.

Whisked Method

This produces sponge-like biscuits as well as those that are crisp and wafer thin. The prepared mixture is either spooned or piped out onto baking sheets. Before the flour is added, the eggs and sugar are whisked together until they are very thick and will support a trail of the mixture for at least 5 seconds. This can be done by hand, with a rotary or balloon whisk, or with a hand-held electric mixer.

Melting Method

This method can be used to produce anything from crisp, melt-in-the-mouth florentines, to harder, crunchier biscuits such as gingersnaps and gingerbread men. The softer mixtures can be spooned out; firmer ones can be hand rolled into balls, or may be rolled out with a rolling pin. This type of dough contains a high sugar content in the form of honey, treacle or syrup as well as sugar, so the dough can be quite sticky when warm, but as it cools it becomes firmer and less sticky, so don't be tempted to knead in extra flour when the dough is warm.

No-bake Biscuits

These are not really true biscuits, but a delicious combination of ingredients which become firm and crisp when they are chilled, producing delightful sweetmeats to serve with coffee, or as an after-dinner petits fours. Although simple and quick to make, they do need long refrigeration for the ingredients to firm up.

Many of the mixtures are bound together with melted chocolate. When melting chocolate, great care should be taken not to overheat it. In some recipes the chocolate is melted in a saucepan over direct heat when it is combined with other ingredients, such as butter and water, but, in most cases it is melted in a double boiler or a bowl over a saucepan of hot water. The bowl should be large enough to fit the top of the saucepan exactly so that water cannot splash up into the chocolate; this would change the texture of the chocolate making it thick and grainy. The bottom of the bowl should not be allowed to touch the water, and the water should be kept at a gentle simmer. Never allow the water to boil.

Once made, no-bake biscuits are best kept in a very cool place or in the refrigerator to prevent them softening. They are particularly good when served slightly chilled.

Meringue-based Biscuits

These include the popular macaroons and amaretti, as well as many other dainty biscuits, perfect for serving with afternoon tea or as petits fours with after-dinner coffee. Although some of the recipes call for the mixture to be piped out, if you are not happy using a piping bag simply spoon the mixture into shape instead.

Refrigerator Biscuits

These are so-called because it is necessary to thoroughly chill the shaped dough before it can be cut into slices for baking, and also because the dough can be conveniently kept in the refrigerator for up to a week before it is baked. Two or three types of refrigerator biscuit dough kept on hand will ensure that you have a never ending supply of biscuits – all speedily made.

Refrigerator biscuit doughs are made by the traditional creaming method and have a high butter and sugar content. The dough is quite soft to handle when it is first made, but after being shaped into rolls, and long refrigeration, it becomes firm enough for cutting into thin slices for baking. These biscuits spread during baking and should be spaced well apart on baking sheets.

BASIC TECHNIQUES

Biscuit making may appear to be a complex affair, but it really isn't if you follow certain simple techniques.

Measuring Ingredients
For perfect results, it is essential to measure very accurately. Spoon measurements throughout the book are all level; dry ingredients should be levelled off with a small knife. Honey, syrup and treacle are the most difficult of all to measure. They should be measured accurately by weighing, or by volume, as tablespoon measures give varying results. The simplest method is to weigh out the sugar first, then increase the weights and spoon the honey, syrup or treacle on top of the sugar. This prevents them sticking to the scale pan. When sugar is not included in the recipe, lightly flouring the scale pan will help prevent honey, and so on, from sticking. Fluid measurements should all be read at eye level, on a level surface.

Preparing Baking Sheets
Every recipe gives definite instructions for the preparation of baking sheets or tins and these instructions should be followed exactly. You may feel that using butter to grease a baking sheet is rather extravagant, but as biscuits have very delicate flavours, which can be very easily spoiled by using a strong-flavoured margarine or lard, butter is recommended. You can, of course, use other fats when lining baking sheets with non-stick baking paper. Greasing the sheet before lining is important to hold the paper in position: especially if you have a fan oven, as the fan does tend to blow the paper up from the baking sheet.

Rolling Out
When rolling out the biscuit doughs you will need to flour both the work surface and the rolling pin to prevent the dough sticking. Use only the barest amount of flour necessary to prevent the dough sticking – if you use too much the dough will become too dry and discolour. Move the dough frequently and flour underneath as you roll it out. Use only the lightest of pressure when rolling out the dough. Too much flour on the surface of doughs spoils their finished appearance, so always brush excess flour off with a small soft pastry brush before cutting out shapes.

Cutting Out
Dip cutters in flour to prevent the dough sticking to them. Cut cleanly through the dough with a firm pressure; do not twist the cutter – this spoils the shape. Remove shapes from work surface to baking sheets with a palette knife – do not be tempted to pick them up with your fingers as they can easily be misshapen.

Baking
All baking times are given as a guide, as most ovens vary in temperature the times may differ a little either way. The type of baking sheet used can also affect the cooking time as some conduct heat better than others and can therefore speed up the baking time.

When removed from the oven, most biscuits will be soft, and should be left on the baking sheet for a few minutes to firm up before being removed to wire racks to cool completely. Biscuits become crisp as they cool. Some biscuits, such as brandy snaps and cigarettes russes have to be removed quickly from the baking sheet so that they can be shaped while still hot. Instructions are given in each recipe as to when and how the biscuits should be removed from baking sheets.

Storing
With a few exceptions, most biscuits keep successfully, provided they are stored correctly in an airtight container – a traditional biscuit tin is best, as it keeps biscuits crisp and and prevents them absorbing moisture from the atmosphere which causes them to soften. Remember to store the container in a cool place.

Firmer-textured, plain biscuits keep for longer then the softer, rich types. As a guide, it is recommended you store plain biscuits for up to 1 week, and the richer types, and those with fillings and icings, for up to 2-3 days. Individual recipes will state if a particular biscuit is nicer eaten the day it is made.

Never store biscuits in the same container as cakes, as they absorb moisture from cakes and lose their crispness.

When packing biscuits for a lunch box, or picnic, wrap them in foil, or put into a separate container to prevent them absorbing flavours and moisture from other foods.

Freezing

A good supply of biscuits – particularly the plainer types – can be kept in the freezer, ready to be baked when unexpected guests arrive, or as required. These are best frozen in their unbaked state, after shaping and cutting out. Open-freeze biscuits until solid on foil-lined baking sheets, then remove from baking sheets and pack in rigid containers for protection. Cover container; label and return to the freezer, and freeze for up to 3 months. Open-freezing biscuits means they remain separate when packed, enabling you to remove just the number you require. To bake, place frozen biscuits on prepared baking sheets and bake from frozen (according to recipe instructions), allowing a few extra minutes cooking time.

Presentation

As with all cooking, it is important to present your biscuits well to make them extra appealing. Serve the daintier types elegantly on china or glass plates, or on small cake stands (with or without a doily). Cookies, savoury and wholefood biscuits are better served in more homely fashion in napkin-lined baskets.

— MALTED BRAN FLAKE BARS —

185 g (6 oz) plain (dark) chocolate, chopped
30 g (1 oz/6 teaspoons) butter
1 tablespoon malt extract
90 g (3 oz/⅔ cup) dried apricots, chopped
60 g (2 oz/⅓ cup) stoned prunes, chopped
90 g (3 oz/3 cups) bran flakes breakfast cereal

Butter a shallow tin measuring about 27.5 x 17.5 cm (11 x 7 in); line base with non-stick paper. Melt chocolate, butter and malt extract together in a bowl placed over a saucepan of gently simmering water.

Add apricots, prunes and bran flakes to chocolate mixture and mix thoroughly. Spread in prepared tin, smoothing top with the back of a spoon. Refrigerate for 1-2 hours until firmly set.

Loosen sides of mixture from tin. Turn out onto a board and remove paper. Turn slab over and cut into 24 pieces: cutting evenly into 3 lengthwise and 8 widthwise. Arrange neatly on a serving dish.

Makes 24.

NUTTY BITES

60 g (2 oz/¼ cup) unsalted butter
60 g (2 oz/2 tablespoons) golden syrup
30 g (1 oz/¼ cup) cocoa
60 g (2 oz/⅓ cup) raisins
60 g (2 oz/½ cup) hazelnuts, toasted and
  chopped
60 g (2 oz/2 cups) cornflakes

Put butter, syrup, cocoa and raisins into a
saucepan and stir over a gentle heat until
melted and well blended.

Stir three-quarters of nuts and the cornflakes
into melted mixture. Spoon mixture into
petits fours cases and sprinkle remaining nuts
over top. Refrigerate for 1 hour until set.

Arrange Nutty Bites attractively on a serving
dish.

Makes 38-40.

Variation: Use chopped glacé cherries and
toasted almonds instead of hazelnuts, if
desired.

EXOTIC TREATS

250 g (8 oz/2 cups) exotic fruit and nut mix
125 g (4 oz) plain (dark) chocolate, chopped
45 g (1½ oz/9 teaspoons) unsalted butter
peel of 2 large oranges, cut into thin slivers

Butter a shallow tin measuring about 27.5 x 17.5 cm (11 x 7 in); line base with non-stick paper. Coarsely grind fruit and nut mix in a food processor or blender.

Melt chocolate and butter together in a bowl placed over a saucepan of gently simmering water, stirring frequently. Mix in half the orange peel and ground nut mix. Spread smoothly in prepared tin and sprinkle with remaining peel, pressing it on lightly. Refrigerate for 1-2 hours until firmly set.

Loosen sides of mixture from tin. Carefully turn out onto a board and remove paper. Turn slab over, then cut into 32 pieces: cutting evenly into 4 lengthwise and 8 widthwise.

Makes 32.

— MUESLI & HONEY COOKIES —

60 g (2 oz/2 tablespoons) clear honey
60 g (2 oz/¼ cup) unsalted butter
125 g (4 oz) plain (dark) chocolate, chopped
250 g (8 oz/2 cups) muesli

Butter a shallow tin measuring 27.5 x 17.5 cm (11 x 7 in); line base with non-stick paper. Melt honey, butter and chocolate together in a large bowl placed over a saucepan of gently simmering water.

Reserve 30 g (1 oz/¼ cup) of muesli. Stir remaining muesli into honey mixture. Spread in prepared tin, smoothing top with the back of a spoon. Sprinkle reserved muesli evenly on top, then press gently into surface of mixture. Refrigerate for 1-2 hours until mixture is firmly set.

Carefully remove muesli slab from tin and remove paper. Cut in half lengthwise, then into 4 widthwise, to make 8 squares. Cut each square in half to make 2 triangles. Arrange neatly on a serving dish.

Makes 16.

— CRÈME DE MENTHE CREAMS —

BASE: 125 g (4 oz/½ cup) unsalted butter
30 g (1 oz/1 tablespoon) golden syrup
375 g (12 oz/3⅓ cups) shortcake biscuit crumbs

FROSTING: 125 g (4 oz/½ cup) unsalted butter
125 ml (4 fl oz/½ cup) double (thick) cream
6 teaspoons crème de menthe
440 g (14 oz/2½ cups) icing sugar, sifted

CHOCOLATE TOPPING: few drops vanilla essence
30 g (1 oz/6 teaspoons) unsalted butter
185 g (6 oz) plain (dark) chocolate, chopped

To make base, melt butter and syrup together in a saucepan, then stir in biscuit crumbs. Spread evenly in a 32.5 x 22.5 cm (13 x 9 in) Swiss roll tin and set aside. To make frosting, heat butter with cream in a large bowl placed over a saucepan of hot water, stirring until butter melts. Stir in crème de menthe and icing sugar and beat until mixture thickens. Spread over base mixture in tin. Refrigerate for 1-2 hours until set.

To make topping, put essence, butter, chocolate and 1 tablespoon cold water into a small bowl and place over a saucepan of gently simmering water, stirring until smooth. Spread chocolate mixture over frosting to cover it completely; mark attractively with a palette knife. Refrigerate until set. When set, cut into 32 pieces: cutting evenly into 4 lengthwise and 8 widthwise.

Makes 32.

LIGHT BARS

2 chocolate coated caramel bars, cut into small pieces
125 g (4 oz) plain (dark) chocolate, chopped
90 g (3 oz/⅓ cup) unsalted butter
90 g (3 oz/3⅔ cups) rice breakfast cereal

Butter a 32.5 x 22.5 cm (13 x 9 in) Swiss roll tin; line base with non-stick paper. Melt caramel bars, chocolate and butter together in a large bowl placed over a saucepan of gently simmering water, stirring frequently until well blended and smooth.

Add rice cereal to chocolate mixture and gently mix together until cereal is well coated. Spread evenly in Swiss roll tin, smoothing top with the back of a spoon. Refrigerate for 1-2 hours until firmly set.

Using a very sharp knife, cut set biscuit mixture into 24 pieces; cutting evenly into 6 lengthwise and 4 widthwise. Carefully remove bars from tin with a small flexible palette knife.

Makes 24.

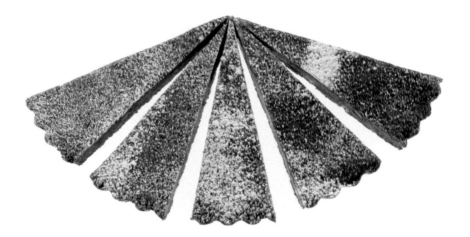

DATE & GINGER FANS

60 g (2 oz/¼ cup) unsalted butter
60 g (2 oz/2 tablespoons) golden syrup
125 g (4 oz) plain (dark) chocolate, chopped
185 g (6 oz/1⅔ cups) digestive biscuit crumbs
90 g (3 oz/½ cup) stoned dates, chopped
60 g (2 oz/⅓ cup) preserved stem ginger,
   chopped

TO FINISH: icing sugar for sifting

Melt butter, syrup and chocolate together in a large bowl placed over a saucepan of gently simmering water, stirring frequently until well blended.

Add biscuits, dates and ginger to chocolate mixture, mix thoroughly together, then spread evenly over base of a 22.5 cm (9 in) loose-bottomed, fluted flan tin. Smooth well with the back of a spoon. Refrigerate for 1-2 hours until firmly set.

Carefully remove side from flan tin. Cut biscuit mixture into 16 even-sized pieces. Using a palette knife, carefully loosen biscuits from base of tin, sift icing sugar over the top, then arrange neatly on a serving plate. Keep refrigerated, or in a cool place, until serving.

Makes 16.

WHISKY MACS

30 g (1 oz/¼ cup) cocoa
60 g (2 oz/2 tablespoons) golden syrup
60 ml (2 fl oz/¼ cup) whisky
90 g (3 oz/⅓ cup) unsalted butter
250 g (8 oz/2¼ cups) ginger biscuit crumbs
125 g (4 oz/1 cup) chopped walnut pieces

TO FINISH: icing sugar for sifting

Line a large baking sheet with foil. Put cocoa,
syrup, whisky and butter into a saucepan and
stir over a low heat until melted and well
blended together.

Stir biscuits and walnuts into whisky
mixture, then allow to cool slightly. Take a
piece of mixture, about the size of a walnut,
roll it into a ball, then flatten to form a neat
round. Place on prepared baking sheet.
Repeat with remaining mixture. Refrigerate
for 1-2 hours until firmly set.

Sift icing sugar lightly over whisky biscuits,
remove from foil and arrange on a serving
plate.

Makes 32.

CALYPSO BARS

250 g (8 oz) white chocolate, chopped
90 g (3 oz/⅓ cup) unsalted butter
60 ml (2 fl oz/¼ cup) dark rum
60 g (2 oz/½ cup) pistachio nuts, skinned
60 g (2 oz/⅓ cup) glacé cherries, roughly
  chopped
125 g (4 oz/1⅓ cups) desiccated coconut
30 g (1 oz) plain (dark) chocolate, melted

Butter a shallow tin measuring about 27.5 x 17.5 cm (11 x 7 in); line base with non-stick paper.

Melt white chocolate, butter and half of rum in a double boiler or a large bowl placed over a pan of gently simmering water, stirring until well blended. Remove from heat, then stir in remaining rum. Roughly chop pistachio nuts; add three-quarters to chocolate, with cherries and coconut. Mix well. Spread mixture evenly in prepared tin.

Finely chop remaining nuts. Put melted plain (dark) chocolate into a small paper piping bag; cut a small hole in bottom of bag. Drizzle lines of melted chocolate all over the top of coconut mixture, then sprinkle with pistachio nuts. Refrigerate for 4-5 hours until firmly set. Cut into 30 bars: cutting evenly into 3 lengthwise and 10 widthwise. Remove from tin with a small flexible palette knife. Keep refrigerated, or in a cool place, until serving.

Makes 30.

BRANDY SNAPS

125 g (4 oz/½ cup) butter
125 g (4 oz/¾ cup) light soft brown sugar
125 g (4 oz/⅓ cup) golden syrup
4 teaspoons lemon juice
4 teaspoons brandy
125 g (4 oz/1 cup) plain flour
1 teaspoon ground ginger

Put butter, sugar, syrup, lemon juice and brandy into a saucepan and stir over a moderate heat until butter melts and sugar dissolves. Remove from heat, sift flour and ginger into pan and mix well. Allow mixture to cool completely.

Preheat oven to 190C (375F/Gas 5). Grease several baking sheets; line with non-stick paper. For ease of handling bake only 6 brandy snaps at a time, placing sheets in oven at 5 minute intervals. Non-stick paper may be re-used; wipe with absorbent kitchen paper before adding more mixture. Drop small teaspoonfuls of mixture onto baking sheets, spaced well apart. Bake in the oven for 8-10 minutes until very lightly browned. Have ready 6 chopsticks or pencils.

Allow brandy snaps to cool for a few seconds, then remove with a palette knife and wrap around chopsticks or pencils. When firm, remove chopsticks or pencils. Place on a tray. Should brandy snaps become too firm to roll up, simply reheat them for a few seconds to soften.

Makes 36.

AMERICAN HERMITS

125 g (4 oz/½ cup) butter
185 g (6 oz/1 cup) light soft brown sugar
1 egg, beaten
60 ml (2 fl oz/¼ cup) thick sour cream
60 ml (2 fl oz/¼ cup) milk
250 g (8 oz/2 cups) plain flour
2 teaspoons baking powder
pinch of salt
2 teaspoons mixed spice
185 g (6 oz/1 cup) raisins

GLAZE: 125 g (4 oz/¾ cup) icing sugar,
    sifted
6 teaspoons single (light) cream
few drops vanilla essence

Preheat oven to 180C (350F/Gas 4). Butter
and flour several baking sheets. In a bowl,
beat butter with sugar until very light. Beat in
egg, thick sour cream and milk. Sift flour,
baking powder, salt and spice into bowl; mix
well. Stir in raisins. Put heaped teaspoonfuls
of mixture on baking sheets; spaced well
apart. Using a fork dipped in cold water,
flatten each mound slightly. Bake in the oven
for 15-18 minutes until lightly browned.

Meanwhile, make glaze. In a small bowl, beat
together icing sugar, cream and vanilla until
smooth. Immediately cookies are removed
from oven, brush glaze thinly over each one.
Place on a wire rack to cool.

Makes 36.

MADELEINES

4 eggs
185 g (6 oz/¾ cup) caster sugar
few drops vanilla essence
½ teaspoon orange flower water
185 g (6 oz/1½ cups) plain flour
125 g (4 oz/½ cup) unsalted butter, melted
and cooled

TO FINISH: caster sugar for sprinkling

Preheat oven to 200C (400F/Gas 6). Butter and flour 1 or 2 Madeleine trays.

Put eggs, sugar, vanilla and orange flower water into a bowl, place over a saucepan of gently simmering water and whisk until very thick. Remove from heat and continue whisking until mixture is cool and will hold the trail of the whisk for 5 seconds. Carefully fold in flour, then gently fold in melted butter.

Three-quarters fill each Madeleine mould with mixture. Bake in the oven for 12-15 minutes until lightly browned and springy to the touch. Remove from moulds onto a wire rack, with shell pattern uppermost. Immediately sprinkle with caster sugar. Continue to bake Madeleines, in batches, until all the mixture is used.

Makes 42.

PETIT LEMON CUPS

30 g (1 oz/6 teaspoons) unsalted butter
30 g (1 oz/5 teaspoons) caster sugar
30 g (1 oz/1 tablespoon) golden syrup
finely grated peel of ½ lemon
30 g (1 oz/¼ cup) plain flour, sifted

FILLING: 45 g (1½ oz/9 teaspoons) unsalted
  butter
finely grated peel of 1 lemon
3 teaspoons lemon juice
1 tablespoon thick sour cream
250 g (8 oz/1½ cups) icing sugar, sifted

Put butter, sugar, syrup and lemon peel into a saucepan and place over moderate heat.

Stir until melted, then stir in flour. Cool. Preheat oven to 190C (375F/Gas 5). Grease a large baking sheet and line with non-stick paper. Using a round ¼ teaspoon measuring spoon, spoon 12 tiny rounds of mixture onto baking sheet, spacing them well apart. Bake in the oven for 5 minutes until lightly browned. Cool for a few seconds. Lift lacy rounds from sheet, then place in tiny bouchée tins to mould into a cup shape.

When cold, remove to a wire rack. Repeat until mixture is used up. To make filling, put butter, lemon peel and juice into a bowl set over a saucepan of gently simmering water and stir until butter melts. Remove from heat. Stir in thick sour cream and icing sugar. Beat until cool and thickened. Spoon, or pipe mixture into centre of each lace cup.

Makes 40.

Note: These are best eaten freshly made.

ITALIAN COOKIES

2 eggs
155 g (5 oz/²⁄₃ cup) caster sugar
finely grated peel of 1 lemon
125 g (4 oz/1 cup) plain flour, sifted
60 g (2 oz/½ cup) pine nuts
60 g (2 oz/⅓ cup) icing sugar

Preheat oven to 180C (350F/Gas 4). Grease several baking sheets; line with non-stick paper. Put eggs, caster sugar and lemon peel into a bowl, place over a saucepan of gently simmering water and whisk until very thick.

Remove from heat. Continue whisking until cool and mixture holds the trail of the whisk for 5 seconds. Very carefully fold in flour. Drop teaspoonfuls of mixture onto baking sheets, spacing them well apart. Sprinkle with pine nuts. Leave to stand for 15 minutes.

Sift icing sugar evenly over cookies, then bake in the oven for 15-20 minutes until lightly browned. Allow to cool on baking sheets for a few minutes, then remove to wire racks to cool completely.

Makes 44.

EGG NOG BROWNIES

2 eggs
1 tablespoon brandy
few drops vanilla essence
125 g (4 oz/½ cup) butter
125 g (4 oz) bitter (unsweetened) chocolate
220 g (7 oz/1 cup) caster sugar
220 g (7 oz/1⅓ cups) light soft brown sugar
155 g (5 oz/1¼ cups) plain flour
125 g (4 oz/1 cup) chopped pecan nuts

Butter a shallow tin measuring about 27.5 x 17.5 x 3 cm (11 x 7 x 1¼ in). Line base with non-stick paper. Preheat oven to 180C (350F/Gas 4).

In a bowl, lightly whisk eggs with brandy and vanilla. Put butter and chocolate into a large saucepan and place over a moderate heat. Stir continuously until melted. Remove from heat; stir in caster and brown sugar, then egg mixture, flour and pecans. Pour into prepared tin and spread evenly. Bake in the oven for 30 minutes or until a cocktail stick inserted into centre comes out clean.

Allow brownie mixture to cool in tin. When cold, cut into 24 small squares: cutting evenly into 4 lengthwise and 6 widthwise. Remove from tin with a small palette knife. Brownies keep well for up to 1 week stored in an airtight tin, in a cool place.

Makes 24.

Note: Brownies are at their best if kept for 2-3 days before serving.

APPLE STREUSEL BARS

BASE: 155 g (5 oz/1¼ cups) plain flour
90 g (3 oz/½ cup) icing sugar
125 g (4 oz/1¼ cups) ground almonds
220 g (7 oz/1 cup) butter
6 tablespoons home-made lemon curd

STREUSEL TOPPING: 1 large red eating apple
90 g (3 oz/⅓ cup) demerara sugar
90 g (3 oz/⅓ cup) butter
185 g (6 oz/1½ cups) plain flour, sifted
1 teaspoon mixed spice

TO FINISH: a little caster sugar for
sprinkling

Preheat oven to 180C (350F/Gas 4). To
make base, sift flour and icing sugar into a
bowl and mix in almonds. Rub in butter until
mixture forms coarse crumbs. Work gently
together to form a soft dough. Roll out on a
floured surface to an oblong a little smaller
than a 32.5 x 22.5 cm (13 x 9 in) Swiss roll
tin. Place mixture in tin and press out to fit.
Smooth top; prick all over with a fork. Spread
lemon curd over base. Refrigerate while
making streusel topping.

Coarsely grate apple; squeeze dry in absorbent
kitchen paper. Put into a bowl with a little
sugar and mix to separate strands. In a bowl,
rub butter into flour until mixture resembles
fine breadcrumbs. Mix in spice, apple and
remaining sugar. Sprinkle evenly over lemon
curd, pressing down lightly. Bake in the oven
for 45-50 minutes until lightly browned.
Cool in tin. When cold, cut into 30 bars.
Dust with caster sugar.

Makes 30.

LEMON SHORTIES

BASE: 250 g (8 oz/1 cup) butter
90 g (3 oz/½ cup) icing sugar, sifted
250 g (8 oz/2 cups) plain flour
60 g (2 oz/⅓ cup) potato flour

LEMON TOPPING: finely grated peel of 3 lemons
250 g (8 oz/1 cup) caster sugar
3 eggs
45 g (1½ oz/⅓ cup) plain flour, sifted
¾ teaspoon baking powder
9 teaspoons strained lemon juice

TO FINISH: icing sugar for sifting

Preheat oven to 180C (350F/Gas 4).

To make base, in a bowl, beat butter and sugar together until creamy. Sift flour and potato flour into bowl and work into butter to form a soft dough. Spread shortbread evenly on base of a 32.5 x 22.5 cm (13 x 9 in) Swiss roll tin. Cover surface with plastic wrap; rub with the back of a spoon to smooth. Remove plastic wrap; prick all over with a fork. Chill for 30 minutes. Bake in the oven for 15-20 minutes until lightly browned. Remove from oven.

To make topping, put lemon peel, sugar and eggs into a bowl, whisk together until smooth and creamy. Sift flour and baking powder into bowl, fold into egg mixture; stir in lemon juice. Pour lemon mixture over shortbread; return to oven for 25 minutes until very lightly browned. Cool in tin. When cold, cut into 30 bars: cutting evenly into 3 lengthwise and 10 widthwise. Sift over icing sugar.

Makes 30.

NUTTY FLAPJACKS

185 g (6 oz/¾ cup) butter
90 g (3 oz/⅓ cup) sugar
90 g (3 oz/¼ cup) black treacle
finely grated peel of 1 large orange
250 g (8 oz/2¾ cups) rolled oats
125 g (4 oz/1 cup) walnuts, chopped

Preheat oven to 200C (400F/Gas 6). Butter a shallow tin measuring about 27.5 x 17.5 x 3 cm (11 x 7 x 1¼ in). Put butter, sugar, treacle and orange peel into a large saucepan; stir continuously over a moderate heat until melted.

Stir oats and walnuts into melted mixture and spoon into prepared tin, then smooth top. Bake in the oven for 20-25 minutes until lightly browned. Remove from oven; allow to cool for 5 minutes, then mark into 20 bars: cutting in half lengthwise, then evenly into 10 widthwise. Leave in tin to cool completely.

Carefully turn flapjacks out of the tin onto a board. Cut through marked divisions once again to form 20 bars.

Makes 20.

LINZERTORTE FINGERS

250 g (8 oz/1½ cups) unblanched almonds
315 g (10 oz/2½ cups) plain flour
pinch of salt
1½ teaspoons mixed spice
155 g (5 oz/1 cup) icing sugar
finely grated peel of 1 large lemon
315 g (10 oz/1¼ cups) unsalted butter, cut
    into small pieces
3 egg yolks
340 g (12 oz) jar raspberry conserve
1 egg
2 teaspoons milk
2 teaspoons caster sugar
60 g (2 oz/½ cup) flaked almonds

Finely grind unblanched almonds.

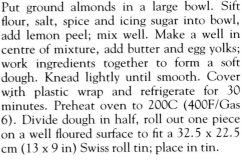

Put ground almonds in a large bowl. Sift flour, salt, spice and icing sugar into bowl, add lemon peel; mix well. Make a well in centre of mixture, add butter and egg yolks; work ingredients together to form a soft dough. Knead lightly until smooth. Cover with plastic wrap and refrigerate for 30 minutes. Preheat oven to 200C (400F/Gas 6). Divide dough in half, roll out one piece on a well floured surface to fit a 32.5 x 22.5 cm (13 x 9 in) Swiss roll tin; place in tin.

Spread jam over pastry. Roll out other half of dough to fit tin, place on top of jam. Lightly whisk egg with milk and sugar and brush over pastry to glaze. Sprinkle with almonds. Bake in the oven for 10 minutes, then lower temperature to 180C (350F/Gas 4) and bake for a further 35 minutes until golden. Cool in tin. When cold, cut into 30 fingers: cutting evenly into 3 lengthwise and 10 widthwise.

Makes 30.

FRUIT FLAPJACKS

185 g (6 oz/¾ cup) butter
60 g (2 oz/¼ cup) demerara sugar
90 g (3 oz/¼ cup) golden syrup
250 g (8 oz/2¾ cups) rolled oats
90 g (3 oz/⅔ cup) dried apricots, chopped
90 g (3 oz/½ cup) stoned dates, chopped
90 g (3 oz/½ cup) stoned prunes, chopped

Preheat oven to 200C (400F/Gas 6). Butter a shallow tin measuring about 27.5 x 17.5 x 3 cm (11 x 7 x 1¼ in). Put butter, sugar and syrup into a large saucepan; stir continuously over a moderate heat until melted.

Stir oats into melted mixture, then spread half over base of tin to form a thin layer. Press with the back of a spoon to firm and smooth. In a bowl, mix apricots, dates and prunes together. Sprinkle evenly over oat mixture, then spread remaining oat mixture on top of fruits; press with spoon to firm and smooth.

Bake in the oven for 20-25 minutes until lightly browned. Allow to cool for 5 minutes, then mark into 24 squares: cutting into 4 lengthwise and 6 widthwise. Leave in tin until completely cold. Re-cut squares, then lift out with a small palette knife.

Makes 24.

—— CARAMEL SHORTBREAD ——

SHORTBREAD: 250 g (8 oz/2 cups) plain flour
pinch of salt
60 g (2 oz/¼ cup) caster sugar
185 g (6 oz/¾ cup) butter

CARAMEL: 125 g (4 oz/½ cup) unsalted butter
400 g (14.1 oz) can condensed milk
2 teaspoons instant coffee granules
60 g (2 oz/¼ cup) caster sugar
60 g (2 oz/2 tablespoons) golden syrup

TOPPING: 185 g (6 oz) plain (dark) chocolate,
   melted
30 g (1 oz) white chocolate, melted

Preheat oven to 180C (350F/Gas 4). To make shortbread, sift flour, salt and sugar into a bowl. Rub in butter until mixture forms coarse crumbs, then work together to form a soft dough. Roll out on a floured surface to an oblong a little smaller than a 32.5 x 22.5 cm (13 x 9 in) Swiss roll tin. Place shortbread in tin; press out to fit. Prick all over with a fork. Chill for 30 minutes. Bake in the oven for 25-30 minutes until lightly browned. Cool.

To make caramel, in a heavy saucepan, stir ingredients over moderate heat until melted. Stirring, bring to a gentle boil; boil until mixture thickens and holds a trail, about 6-8 minutes. Spread over shortbread. Cool. Spread plain chocolate over caramel. Put white chocolate into a paper piping bag, cut a small hole in bag; pipe lines across plain chocolate, 1 cm (½ in) apart. Pull a skewer through lines to decorate. Cut into squares when set.

Makes 48.

— CHOC & RAISIN SHORTIES —

220 g (7 oz/1¾ cups) plain flour
pinch of salt
30 g (1 oz/8 teaspoons) potato flour
60 g (2 oz/¼ cup) vanilla sugar
185 g (6 oz/¾ cup) butter
60 g (2 oz/⅓ cup) raisins, chopped
250 g (8 oz) plain (dark) cake covering chocolate,
  chopped

Preheat oven to 180C (350F/Gas 4). Sift flour, salt, potato flour and vanilla sugar into a bowl. Rub in butter until mixture forms coarse crumbs, then mix in raisins. Work together to form a soft dough.

Roll out dough on a floured surface to an oblong a little smaller than a 27.5 x 17.5 x 3 cm (11 x 7 x 1¼ in) tin. Place dough in tin and press out to fit. Smooth top; prick all over with a fork. Bake for 25-30 minutes until very lightly browned. Allow to cool for a few minutes. Using a sharp knife, mark shortbread into 28 .squares: cutting evenly into 4 lengthwise and 7 widthwise. Cool in tin.

Re-cut shortbread squares. Melt chocolate in a double boiler or a bowl over a pan of gently simmering water; stir until smooth. Line a baking sheet with foil. Dip shortbread squares in chocolate to coat evenly, then lift out with a fork and tap on side of bowl to remove excess chocolate. Place on foil. Leave in a cool place to set. If desired, any remaining chocolate may be used to decorate.

Makes 28.

CHERRY PRALINE RINGS

60 g (2 oz/½ cup) hazelnuts, skinned
155 g (5 oz/⅔ cup) caster sugar
125 g (4 oz/½ cup) butter
1 egg
375 g (12 oz/3 cups) plain flour
pinch of salt
1 teaspoon baking powder
185 g (6 oz/1 cup) glacé cherries,
   halved and thinly sliced

GLAZE: 1 small egg, beaten
3 teaspoons milk
2 teaspoons caster sugar

TO FINISH: caster sugar for sprinkling

Lightly oil a small baking sheet. Put nuts and 60 g (2 oz/¼ cup) sugar into a small saucepan; stir over low heat until sugar caramelizes. Pour onto baking sheet. When cold, break up and grind finely, then sieve. Preheat oven to 180C (350F/Gas 4). Grease several baking sheets. In a bowl, cream butter with remaining sugar. Beat in egg, then sieved praline. Sift flour, salt and baking powder into mixture; blend in with spoon, then work by hand to form a dough. Knead lightly until smooth.

Roll out dough on floured surface to 0.3 cm (⅛ in) thick. Using a 6 cm (2½ in) fluted cutter, cut out rounds from dough; remove centres with a 1 cm (½ in) cutter. Place rings, slightly apart, on baking sheets. Re-knead and re-roll trimmings to make 38-40 rings in total. Mix glaze ingredients together; brush over rings. Decorate with cherries. Bake for 15-20 minutes until lightly browned. Sprinkle with sugar. Cool on wire racks.

Makes 38-40.

SHREWSBURY BISCUITS

155 g (5 oz/²⁄₃ cup) butter
155 g (5 oz/²⁄₃ cup) caster sugar
1 egg
few drops vanilla essence
375 g (12 oz/3 cups) plain flour
1 teaspoon baking powder
pinch of salt

In a bowl, beat butter with sugar until creamy. Beat in egg and vanilla to taste. Sift flour, baking powder and salt into bowl; blend in with spoon, then work by hand to form a dough. Knead lightly until smooth.

Wrap dough in plastic wrap or greaseproof paper. Chill for 45 minutes. Grease several baking sheets. Roll out dough on a floured surface to 0.3 cm (⅛ in) thick. Using a 6 cm (2 ½ in) fluted cutter, cut out as many rounds as possible from dough. Place, slightly apart, on baking sheets. Re-knead and re-roll trimmings: cut out more rounds to make 44 in total. Refrigerate for 30 minutes. Preheat oven to 180C (350F/Gas 4).

Bake biscuits in the oven for 15-20 minutes until very lightly coloured. Using a palette knife, carefully remove biscuits from baking sheets to wire racks to cool.

Makes 44.

Note: These biscuits can be sprinkled with icing sugar after baking, if desired.

SABLÉS

155 g (5 oz/1¼ cups) plain flour
pinch of salt
60 g (2 oz/¼ cup) caster sugar
60 g (2 oz/½ cup) finely ground almonds
finely grated peel of 1 lemon
90 g (3 oz/⅓ cup) butter
2 egg yolks

TO FINISH: icing sugar for sifting

Butter several baking sheets. Sift flour, salt and sugar into a bowl, mix in almonds and lemon peel. Rub in butter until mixture resembles fine breadcrumbs, then mix in egg yolks to form a soft dough.

Roll out dough on a floured surface to 0.3 cm (⅛ in) thick. Using an oblong biscuit roller, cut 32 oblongs from dough. Alternatively, cut biscuits by hand with a knife, or pastry wheel: cutting into long strips 7.5 cm (3 in) wide, then cutting across strips at 4.5 cm (1¾ in) intervals to form oblongs. Place, slightly apart, on baking sheets. Refrigerate for 30 minutes. Preheat oven to 180C (350F/Gas 4).

Bake Sablés in the oven for 15-20 minutes until very lightly browned. Using a palette knife, carefully remove biscuits from baking sheets to wire racks to cool. When cold, sift very lightly with icing sugar.

Makes 32.

SUGAR & SPICE BISCUITS

250 g (8 oz/2 cups) plain flour
pinch of salt
½ teaspoon ground cinnamon
¼ teaspoon ground allspice
¼ teaspoon ground mace
¼ teaspoon ground cloves
½ teaspoon baking powder
125 g (4 oz/½ cup) caster sugar
125 g (4 oz/½ cup) butter
1 egg, beaten

GLAZE: 1 small egg, beaten
3 teaspoons milk
2 teaspoons caster sugar
6 teaspoons granulated sugar

Butter several baking sheets. Sift flour, salt, spices, baking powder and sugar into a bowl. Rub in butter until mixture resembles fine breadcrumbs. Stir in egg; mix by hand to form a soft dough. Roll out dough on a floured surface to 0.3 cm (⅛ in) thick. Using fancy biscuit cutters, cut out as many shapes as possible from dough. Place on baking sheets. Re-knead and re-roll trimmings; cut out more shapes to make 32 in total. Refrigerate shapes for 30 minutes. Preheat oven to 180C (350F/Gas 4).

To make glaze, stir together egg, milk and caster sugar in a small bowl. Brush glaze over each biscuit, then sprinkle with half the granulated sugar. Bake in the oven for 15-20 minutes until lightly browned. Remove from oven and immediately sprinkle with remaining granulated sugar. Using a palette knife, carefully remove biscuits from sheets to wire racks to cool.

Makes 32.

HAZELNUT SPECULAAS

250 g (8 oz/2 cups) hazelnuts
125 g (4 oz/1¼ cups) ground almonds
185 g (6 oz/¾ cup) caster sugar
185 g (6 oz/1 cup) icing sugar, sifted
2 teaspoons lemon juice
1 egg, beaten

SPICY DOUGH: 250 g (8 oz/2 cups) plain flour
¾ teaspoon baking powder
1 teaspoon mixed spice
90 g (3 oz/½ cup) light soft brown sugar
125 g (4 oz/½ cup) butter
2 small eggs
1 tablespoon milk
2 teaspoons caster sugar
20 blanched almonds, split into halves

Skin hazelnuts, then lightly toast nuts and grind finely. Put hazelnuts into a bowl with almonds and sugars; mix well. Mix with lemon juice and egg to make a firm paste. On a surface sifted with icing sugar, knead paste until smooth. Divide in half; shape each piece into a neat roll, about 30 cm (12 in) long. Wrap and chill for 30 minutes.

To make dough, sift flour, baking powder, spice and sugar into a bowl; rub in butter until mixture resembles fine breadcrumbs. Mix with 1 beaten egg to form a dough; knead lightly until smooth. Wrap and chill for 30 minutes. Preheat oven to 180C (350F/Gas 4). Butter a large baking sheet.

Roll out dough on lightly floured surface to a square a little larger than 30 cm (12 in) and trim edges to neaten. Cut in half to make two 15 cm (6 in) wide strips. Beat remaining egg, then brush over pastry strips. Place a roll of hazelnut paste on each strip; roll up neatly to enclose. Place rolls on baking sheet with joins underneath.

Mix remaining beaten egg with milk and caster sugar. Brush rolls with glaze. Decorate with almonds, placed slightly at an angle, in a long line on top. Brush almonds with glaze.

Bake in the oven for 30-35 minutes until golden. Using 2 large palette knives, very carefully remove rolls from baking sheet to a wire rack to cool. When cold, cut each roll, diagonally, into thin slices, cutting between almonds.

Makes 40.

ALMOND FLOWERS

250 g (8 oz/2¼ cups) ground almonds
125 g (4 oz/½ cup) caster sugar
125 g (4 oz/¾ cup) icing sugar, sifted
1 teaspoon rose water
1 teaspoon orange flower water
few drops almond essence
3 egg yolks

GLAZE: 60 g (2 oz/¼ cup) caster sugar
9 teaspoons warm water
2 egg yolks

TO DECORATE: 12 walnut quarters
7 blanched almonds, split into halves
8 skinned pistachio nuts, split into halves

In a bowl, mix ground almonds with sugars and make a well in centre. Add flavourings and egg yolks and mix to form a stiff paste. Knead lightly until smooth. Wrap in plastic wrap. Set aside. To make glaze, dissolve sugar with 1 tablespoon cold water in small saucepan. Boil to a caramel. Add warm water and heat to dissolve. Cool, then whisk in yolks. Preheat oven to 230C (450F/Gas 8). Line several baking sheets with non-stick paper.

Roll out almond paste to 0.5 cm (¼ in) thick. Using a 5 cm (2 in) flower cutter, stamp out as many flower shapes as possible. Re-knead and re-roll trimmings: cut out more shapes to make 42 in total. Place on baking sheets. Brush with glaze. Decorate with nuts. Bake in the oven for 5 minutes until browned. Cool on baking sheets.

Makes 42.

PINWHEELS

185 g (6 oz/¾ cup) butter
185 g (6 oz/¾ cup) caster sugar
few drops vanilla essence
2 eggs
560 g (1 lb 2 oz/4½ cups) plain flour
2 teaspoons baking powder
salt
1 teaspoon brandy
2 tablespoons cocoa
1 egg white, very lightly beaten

Divide butter and sugar equally between 2 bowls.

To make vanilla dough, beat one portion of butter and sugar until creamy; beat in vanilla to taste and 1 egg. Sift half the flour, 1 teaspoon baking powder and a pinch of salt into bowl. Blend in with spoon, then work by hand to form dough. Wrap; chill 45 minutes. Make chocolate dough in same way with remaining butter, sugar and egg, adding brandy and sifting cocoa in with remaining flour and baking powder. Wrap and chill 45 minutes. Roll out doughs separately on a floured surface to oblongs about 32.5 x 27.5 cm (13 x 11 in).

Brush vanilla dough with egg white; place chocolate dough on top. Trim edges to neaten. Brush chocolate dough with egg white. Roll up, from one long side, to form a tight roll. Wrap and chill for 1 hour. Preheat oven to 180C (350F/Gas 4). Butter several baking sheets. Cut roll into 0.5 cm (¼ in) thick slices; place on baking sheets. Bake in the oven for 20 minutes until lightly browned. Remove to wire racks to cool.

Makes 48.

CHOCOLATE PRETZELS

60 g (2 oz) bitter (unsweetened) chocolate
125 g (4 oz/½ cup) butter
125 g (4 oz/½ cup) caster sugar
few drops vanilla essence
1 egg
280 g (9 oz/2¼ cups) plain flour
pinch of salt
½ teaspoon baking powder
1 small egg white, lightly beaten
2 tablespoons demerara sugar

Melt chocolate in a double boiler or a small bowl placed over a saucepan of simmering water. Cool.

In a bowl, beat butter with caster sugar until creamy. Beat in vanilla to taste, egg and melted chocolate. Sift flour, salt and baking powder into bowl. Blend in with a spoon, then work by hand to form a smooth dough. Wrap in plastic wrap. Chill for 45 minutes. Butter several baking sheets. Divide chilled dough into pieces about the size of a small walnut, or 15 g (½ oz) each.

To shape pretzels, roll pieces of dough into thin strands about 27.5 cm (11 in) long: taking each end, curve round to form a loop, crossing ends over. Take ends back up to top of loop: press firmly in position to secure. Place on baking sheets. Chill 30 minutes. Preheat oven to 180C (350F/Gas 4). Lightly brush pretzels with egg white; sprinkle with demerara sugar. Bake in the oven for 15-20 minutes. Cool on wire racks.

Makes about 42.

GINGERBREAD MEN

500 g (1 lb/4 cups) plain flour
pinch of salt
2 teaspoons ground ginger
1 teaspoon mixed spice
2 teaspoons bicarbonate of soda
125 g (4 oz/½ cup) butter
60 g (2 oz/⅓ cup) light soft brown sugar
60 g (2 oz/¼ cup) caster sugar
90 g (3 oz/¼ cup) black treacle
60 g (2 oz/2 tablespoons) golden syrup
1 egg, beaten

Preheat oven to 180C (350F/Gas 4). Butter several baking sheets. Sift dry ingredients into a bowl and make a well in centre.

Put butter, sugars, treacle and syrup into a saucepan and stir over moderate heat until melted. Pour into flour. Add egg and mix to form a dough. On a floured surface, knead lightly until smooth. Roll out to 0.3 cm (⅛ in) thick. Using a gingerbread man cutter, cut out as many shapes as possible from dough. Place on baking sheets. Re-knead and re-roll trimmings: cut out more shapes. Continue until dough is used up to make 23-24 gingerbread men in total.

Bake in the oven for 20 minutes until lightly browned. Allow to cool on baking sheets for a few minutes, then remove to wire racks to cool completely. Traditionally, gingerbread men are left plain, but if desired they may be decorated as simply or as elaborately as you choose: royal icing, glacé icing and bought edible decorations are all suitable.

Makes 23-24.

OZNEI HAMAN

125 g (4 oz/½ cup) butter
125 g (4 oz/½ cup) caster sugar
few drops vanilla essence
3 egg yolks, plus beaten egg for brushing
250 g (8 oz/2 cups) plain flour
pinch of salt

POPPY SEED FILLING: 45 g (1½ oz/⅓ cup)
   poppy seeds, finely ground
1 tablespoon honey
30 g (1 oz/5 teaspoons) caster sugar
finely grated peel of ½ lemon
1 tablespoon lemon juice
45 g (1½ oz/⅓ cup) ground almonds
1 small egg
30 g (1 oz/¼ cup) raisins

In a bowl, beat butter with sugar until creamy, then beat in vanilla to taste and egg yolks. Sift flour and salt into bowl; blend in with a spoon, then work by hand to form a dough. Knead lightly until smooth. Wrap in plastic wrap and chill whilst making filling. To make filling, put poppy seeds, 60 ml (2 fl oz/¼ cup) water, honey, sugar, lemon peel and juice in a saucepan. Bring to the boil, stirring.

Beat almonds, egg and raisins into poppy seed mixture. Cool. Preheat oven to 180C (350F/ Gas 4). Butter 2 baking sheets. Roll out dough, on a floured surface, to 0.3 cm (⅛ in) thick. Cut out 7.5 cm (3 in) rounds. Put a teaspoonful of poppy seed mixture on each round. Brush edges with beaten egg, then bring edges to centre to cover filling and form a tricorn shape. Place on baking sheets. Glaze with egg. Bake in the oven for 20-35 minutes. Cool on wire racks.

Makes 22.

LITTLE GEMS

90 g (3 oz/⅓ cup) butter
60 g (2 oz/⅓ cup) icing sugar, sifted
1 egg yolk
125 g (4 oz/1 cup) plain flour
pinch of salt

ICING: 1 egg white
250 g (8 oz/1½ cups) icing sugar, sifted
few drops assorted food colourings

In a bowl, cream butter with icing sugar; beat in egg yolk. Sift flour and salt into bowl; blend in with a spoon, then work by hand to form a smooth dough. Wrap and chill for 30 minutes.

Preheat oven to 180C (350F/Gas 4). Butter 2 large baking sheets. Roll out dough on a floured surface to 0.3 cm (⅛ in) thick. Using a 2 cm (¾ in) fluted cutter, cut out as many rounds as possible; place on baking sheets. Re-roll and re-knead trimmings and cut out more rounds to make 110 in total. Bake in the oven for 8-10 minutes until very lightly browned. Remove from baking sheets to wire racks to cool.

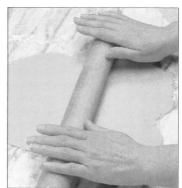

To make icing, in a bowl, lightly whisk egg white. Beat in icing sugar, beating until very white and icing holds stiff peaks. Divide icing between 3 or 4 small bowls and add a few drops of a different food colouring to each one. Put icings in small paper piping bags, each one fitted with a small star nozzle. Pipe a rosette of icing on each biscuit. Allow to dry.

Makes 110.

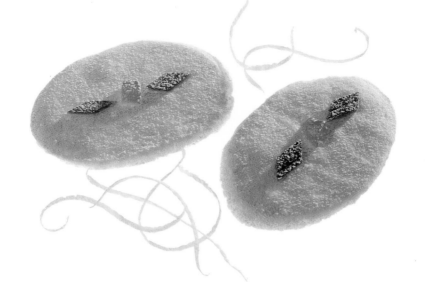

HARPTREE BISCUITS

185 g (6 oz/¾ cup) unsalted butter
90 g (3 oz/½ cup) icing sugar, sifted
finely grated peel of 1 lemon
220 g (7 oz/1¾ cups) plain flour
pinch of salt

TO DECORATE: 5-6 glacé cherries, cut into small
    pieces, if desired
80 small angelica 'leaves', if desired

TO FINISH: icing sugar for sifting

In a bowl, beat butter with icing sugar until
very light and fluffy, then beat in lemon peel.

Sift the flour and salt into bowl and work in
by hand to form a soft dough. On a floured
surface, knead lightly until smooth, then
shape into a thick roll, about 30 cm (12 in)
long. Wrap in plastic wrap and refrigerate for
4-5 hours, or overnight. (The roll may also be
stored in the refrigerator for up to 1 week
before baking.) Preheat oven to 180C (350F/
Gas 4). Butter several baking sheets.

Cutting diagonally, cut chilled dough into
thin slices, about 0.5 cm (¼) thick. Place on
baking sheets. If desired, decorate each
biscuit with a small piece of cherry and
angelica 'leaves'. Bake in the oven for 15-20
minutes until just slightly coloured. Allow to
cool on baking sheets for a few minutes, then
remove to wire racks to cool completely.
When cold, sift lightly with icing sugar.

Makes 40.

MOCHA BISCUITS

375 g (12 oz/1½ cups) unsalted butter
375 g (12 oz/1½ cups) caster sugar
1 egg
few drops vanilla essence
1 teaspoon coffee granules, dissolved in 2 teaspoons
    boiling water
30 g (1 oz) bitter (unsweetened) chocolate, melted
470 g (15 oz/3¾ cups) plain flour
salt

In a bowl, beat butter with sugar until very light and fluffy. Beat in egg.

Divide creamed mixture evenly between 3 bowls, allowing about 250 g (8 oz) to each bowl. Beat vanilla to taste into 1 bowl; cooled coffee mixture into second bowl and cooled, melted chocolate into third bowl. Sift 155 g (5 oz/1¼ cups) flour and a pinch of salt into each bowl. Blend each mixture separately with a spoon, then work by hand to form a dough. On a floured surface, lightly knead each portion of dough until smooth. Shape each one into a long smooth roll, about 45 cm (18 in) long.

Place vanilla and coffee rolls side-by-side. Place chocolate roll, down centre, on top. Press all 3 rolls gently together. Cut in half; wrap in plastic wrap. Refrigerate for 3-4 hours, or overnight. Preheat oven to 180C (350F/Gas 4). Butter several baking sheets. Cut chilled rolls into 0.5 cm (¼ in) thick slices. Place on baking sheets. Bake in the oven for 15-18 minutes until lightly brown. Cool on wire racks.

Makes 72.

JAMAICA CRUNCHIES

250 g (8 oz/1 cup) unsalted butter
185 g (6 oz/1 cup) light soft brown sugar
4 teaspoons dark rum
220 g (7 oz/1¾ cups) plain flour
pinch of salt
60 g (2 oz/½ cup) ground almonds
90 g (3 oz/½ cup) blanched almonds, lightly
    toasted and finely chopped
90 g (3 oz/1 cup) desiccated coconut

In a bowl, beat butter with sugar until light and fluffy. Beat in rum. Sift flour and salt into a bowl. Add ground and chopped almonds. Mix to form a dough.

On a floured surface, lightly knead dough until smooth. Shape into a smooth roll, about 37.5 cm (15 in) long. Wrap in plastic wrap and refrigerate for 3-4 hours, or overnight.

Preheat oven to 180C (350F/Gas 4). Butter several baking sheets. Cut chilled dough into 0.5 cm (¼ in) thick slices. Place on baking sheets. Sprinkle two-thirds of coconut over biscuits to give an even covering. Bake in the oven for 15-20 minutes until very lightly browned. Immediately biscuits are removed from oven, sprinkle with remaining coconut. Remove from baking sheets to wire racks to cool.

Makes 60.

LANGUES DE CHAT

60 g (2 oz/¼ cup) butter
90 g (3 oz/⅓ cup) caster sugar
1 egg, beaten
60 g (2 oz/½ cup) plain flour

Preheat oven to 220C (425F/Gas 7). Grease several baking sheets; line with non-stick paper. In a bowl, beat butter with sugar until very light and fluffy. Gradually beat in egg. Sift flour into bowl and fold in to form a soft dough.

Put mixture into a piping bag fitted with a 10 mm (⅜ in) plain nozzle. Pipe 7.5 cm (3 in) lengths of mixture on baking sheets, cutting dough off at nozzle with a small knife when required length is reached. Space very well apart as biscuits will spread.

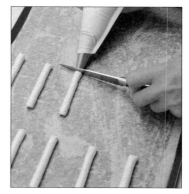

Bake in the oven for 6-8 minutes until golden brown around edges. Allow to cool on baking sheets for a few minutes. Using a palette knife, very carefully remove to a wire rack to cool.

Makes 36-40.

VIENNESE FINGERS

250 g (8 oz/1 cup) butter
60 g (2 oz/⅓ cup) icing sugar, sifted
few drops vanilla essence
250 g (8 oz/2 cups) plain flour
pinch of salt
15 g (½ oz/1 tablespoon) pistachio nuts,
   skinned and chopped

TO FINISH: 60 g (2 oz) plain (dark) cake covering
   chocolate, chopped

Preheat oven to 180C (350F/Gas 4). Butter several baking sheets and dust lightly with flour.

In a bowl, beat butter with icing sugar until very light and creamy. Beat in vanilla to taste. Sift flour and salt into bowl; work into mixture with a wooden spoon to form a soft dough. Put into a piping bag fitted with a 1 cm (½ in) 10 point star nozzle. Pipe 6 cm (2½ in) lengths of mixture on baking sheets, spaced apart, cutting mixture off at nozzle with a small knife when required length is reached. Sprinkle with pistachio nuts.

Bake in the oven for 20-25 minutes until very lightly browned. Cool on baking sheets for a few minutes, then remove to wire racks to cool completely. Melt chocolate in a double boiler or a small bowl placed over a saucepan of simmering water; stir until smooth. Dip both ends of biscuits in melted chocolate, scraping off excess on side of bowl. Place on foil. Leave in a cool place until set.

Makes 24.

OYSTER BISCUITS

250 g (8 oz/1 cup) butter
60 g (2 oz/⅓ cup) icing sugar, sifted
220 g (7 oz/1¾ cups) plain flour
pinch of salt
30 g (1 oz/3 tablespoons) custard powder
15 glacé cherries, cut into halves

TO FINISH: icing sugar for sifting

Preheat oven to 180C (350F/Gas 4). Butter several baking sheets; dust lightly with flour. In a bowl, beat butter with icing sugar until very light and creamy.

Sift flour, salt and custard powder into bowl and work into mixture with a wooden spoon to form a soft dough. Put into a piping bag fitted with a 1 cm (½ in) 10 point star nozzle. Pipe 30 shell shapes on baking sheets, spaced well apart. Place half a cherry on pointed end of each shell.

Bake in the oven for 20-25 minutes until very lightly browned. Allow to cool on baking sheets for a few minutes, then remove to wire racks to cool completely. When cold, sift icing sugar lightly over biscuits.

Makes 30.

VIENNESE WHIRLS

185 g (6 oz/¾ cup) unsalted butter
45 g (1½ oz/3 tablespoons) icing sugar, sifted
few drops vanilla essence
1 teaspoon Grand Marnier
185 g (6 oz/1½ cups) plain flour
pinch of salt

TO FINISH: icing sugar for sifting
1-2 teaspoons red jam

Preheat oven to 180C (350F/Gas 4). Place 12-16 paper baking cases in deep bun tin trays.

In a bowl, beat butter with icing sugar until very light and fluffy. Beat in vanilla to taste and Grand Marnier. Sift flour and salt into bowl and work into mixture with a wooden spoon to form a soft dough. Put mixture into a piping bag fitted with a 1 cm (½ in) 10 point star nozzle. Pipe a whirl of mixture into each paper case, starting at centre and working outwards.

Bake in the oven for 20-25 minutes until very lightly browned. Carefully remove to a wire rack to cool. When cold, very lightly sift icing sugar over each whirl. Spoon, or pipe a small blob of jam in the centre of each one.

Makes 12-16.

FINE SCROLL BISCUITS

60 g (2 oz/¼ cup) unsalted butter
125 g (4 oz/½ cup) caster sugar
few drops vanilla essence
3 egg whites
60 g (2 oz/½ cup) plain flour
6 teaspoons melted butter, cooled

Preheat oven to 180C (350F/Gas 4). Butter several baking sheets. Have ready 6 clean chopsticks or pencils.

In a bowl, beat butter with sugar until creamy. Beat in vanilla to taste. Gradually beat in egg whites. Sift flour into bowl and stir into creamed mixture until smooth. Mix in cooled butter. Spoon mixture into a piping bag, fitted with a 10 mm (⅜ in) plain nozzle. Pipe 6 mounds, about 4 cm (1½ in) in diameter, on each baking sheet, spaced very well apart. Spread each mound out thinly to a circle about 7.5 cm (3 in) in diameter.

Bake 1 sheet of mixture at a time, for 5-6 minutes until golden brown around edges. Remove from oven. Immediately, remove mounds from baking sheet with a palette knife and quickly roll each one around a chopstick or pencil. Place on a wire rack to cool; removing chopsticks or pencils as soon as cigarettes hold their shape. Repeat with remaining mixture.

Makes 28-30.

TRIPLE ORANGE DROPS

60 g (2 oz/¼ cup) unsalted butter
60 g (2 oz/¼ cup) caster sugar
finely grated peel of 1 small orange
1 teaspoon Grand Marnier
1 egg, beaten
60 g (2 oz/½ cup) plain flour
15 g (½ oz/1 tablespoon) finely chopped
    candied orange peel

GLAZE: 2 tablespoons orange marmalade, heated
    and sieved
60 g (2 oz/⅓ cup) icing sugar, sifted
1 teaspoon Grand Marnier
2 teaspoons fresh orange juice

Preheat oven to 220C (425F/Gas 7). Butter 2 baking sheets. In a bowl, beat butter with sugar and orange peel until creamy. Beat in Grand Marnier, then gradually beat in egg. Sift flour into bowl, add peel and stir into creamed mixture until smooth. Put into a piping bag fitted with a 1 cm (½ in) plain nozzle. Pipe rounds of mixture, about 4 cm (1½ in) in diameter, on baking sheets, spaced well apart. Bake in the oven for 6-8 minutes until golden brown around edges and dry in centre.

Meanwhile, make glaze. Heat marmalade in a small saucepan until boiling. In a small bowl, blend icing sugar with Grand Marnier and orange juice to make a thin icing. Immediately orange drops are removed from oven, brush each one with marmalade and then with icing, to glaze evenly. Return to oven for 30 seconds to set glaze. Using a palette knife, very carefully remove from baking sheets to wire racks to cool.

Makes 24.

BRANDY SHAPES

125 g (4 oz/½ cup) butter
185 g (6 oz/¾ cup) caster sugar
2 teaspoons brandy
1 egg, beaten
250 g (8 oz/2 cups) plain flour
pinch of salt

TO DECORATE: 14 raisins
icing sugar for sifting
60 g (2 oz/⅓ cup) icing sugar, sifted
3 teaspoons lemon juice
lemon jelly slices, cut into fans

Preheat oven to 190C (375F/Gas 5). Butter
several baking sheets. In a bowl, beat butter
with sugar until very creamy.

Beat in brandy. Gradually beat in egg. Sift
flour and salt into bowl; work in with a
wooden spoon to form a fairly stiff dough. Put
mixture into a piping bag, fitted with a 1 cm
(½ in) 10 point star nozzle. Pipe half the
mixture onto baking sheets in 'S' shapes,
about 5 cm (2 in) long, spaced well apart.
Decorate with raisins. Pipe remaining
mixture into rings.

Bake in the oven for 15-20 minutes until
lightly browned. Remove from baking sheets
to wire racks to cool. To decorate, sift icing
sugar very lightly over 'S' shapes. In a small
bowl, blend measured icing sugar with lemon
juice to make a thin icing. Brush over rings;
decorate with lemon fans before icing sets.

Makes 27-28.

CINNAMON FINGERS

2 egg whites
250 g (8 oz/1 ¼ cups) caster sugar
4 teaspoons potato flour
2 teaspoons ground cinnamon
185 g (6 oz/1 ¼ cups) ground almonds
30 g (1 oz/⅓ cup) desiccated coconut

Preheat oven to 180C (350F/Gas 4). Grease several baking sheets; line with non-stick paper. In a bowl, whisk egg whites until stiff. Sift sugar, potato flour and cinnamon into bowl; add ground almonds.

Mix gently together to form a stiff paste. Put into a piping bag, fitted with a 10 mm (⅜ in) plain nozzle and pipe 7.5 cm (3 in) lengths of mixture on baking sheets, spaced well apart. Sprinkle evenly with coconut.

Bake in the oven for 25 minutes until lightly browned. Allow to cool on baking sheets for a few minutes, then remove to wire racks to cool completely.

Makes 40.

SPRITZ COOKIES

250 g (8 oz/1 cup) butter
250 g (8 oz/1¼ cups) caster sugar
few drops vanilla essence
2 eggs
440 g (14 oz/3½ cups) plain flour
pinch of salt

TO DECORATE: glacé cherries, angelica
  'leaves', small pieces of glacé fruit, chopped
  nuts, if desired

TO FINISH: caster sugar, coloured sugars, icing
  sugar, if desired

Preheat oven to 190C (375F/Gas 5). Lightly
butter several baking sheets. In a bowl, beat
butter with caster sugar until creamy; beat in
vanilla to taste and eggs. Sift flour and salt
into bowl, then mix in with a wooden spoon
to form a fairly stiff dough. Fill a cookie press
with dough: the simplest way being to first
shape dough, on a floured surface, into rolls.
Press out desired shapes onto baking sheets.

Cookies may be decorated before baking with
small pieces of cherry, angelica 'leaves', glacé
fruits or nuts, as desired. Bake in the oven for
12-15 minutes until very lightly browned.
Remove from baking sheets to wire racks to
cool. To finish after baking, cookies may be
sprinkled with caster sugar or coloured sugars
immediately they are removed from oven.
When cold, they may be sifted with icing
sugar.

Makes 120.

SPICED SPRITZ COOKIES

125 g (4 oz/½ cup) butter
125 g (4 oz/¾ cup) icing sugar, sifted
finely grated peel of 1 lemon
1 egg
250 g (8 oz/2 cups) plain flour
pinch of salt
2 teaspoons ground ginger

Preheat oven to 190C (375F/Gas 5). Lightly butter several baking sheets. In a bowl, beat butter with icing sugar and lemon peel until creamy; beat in egg.

Sift flour, salt and ginger into bowl; mix in with a wooden spoon to form a fairly stiff dough. Fill a cookie press with dough. Press out desired shapes onto baking sheets. Bake in the oven for 12-15 minutes until very lightly browned. Remove from baking sheets to wire racks to cool.

Makes 60.

Variations: Sift in 2 teaspoons mixed spice with flour; add finely grated peel of 1 orange to the creamed butter or add 60 g (2 oz) bitter (unsweetened) chocolate, melted and cooled, after beating in eggs. Leave cookies plain, or decorate as for Spritz Cookies, see page 63. Two-tone cookies may be made by filling cookie tube with a plain dough and a chocolate dough: 2 rolls of mixture placed side-by-side in tube.

COCONUT SANDWICHES

2 egg whites
185 g (6 oz/¾ cup) caster sugar
4 teaspoons potato flour
185 g (6 oz/2 cups) desiccated coconut

FILLING: 30 g (1 oz/6 teaspoons) unsalted
    butter
30 g (1 oz/1 tablespoon) golden syrup
125 ml (4 fl oz/½ cup) condensed milk
few drops vanilla essence

Preheat oven to 180C (350F/Gas 4). Grease several baking sheets; line with non-stick paper.

In a bowl, whisk egg whites until stiff, then fold in sugar, potato flour and coconut. Gently squeeze mixture together to form a soft paste. Roll out on a surface lightly sifted with potato flour to 0.5 cm (¼ in) thick. Using a 5 cm (2 in) plain round cutter, stamp out rounds. Place on baking sheets, spaced well apart. Squeeze trimmings together, re-roll, then stamp out more rounds. Continue until mixture is used up to make 24-28 in total.

Bake in the oven for 20-25 minutes until only just lightly browned. Allow to cool on baking sheets. To make filling, put ingredients in a small heavy-based saucepan. Place pan over a moderate heat and stir continuously until mixture thickens enough to hold a trail for a few seconds. Take care not to let caramel burn. Sandwich biscuits together with caramel.

Makes 12-14.

— ORANGE CHOCOLATE RINGS —

125 g (4 oz/½ cup) butter
125 g (4 oz/¾ cup) light soft brown sugar
1 egg, beaten
250 g (8 oz/2 cups) plain flour
½ teaspoon baking powder
pinch of salt

TO COAT: 185 g (6 oz) plain (dark) cake covering
  chocolate, melted

FILLING: 45 g (1½ oz/9 teaspoons) unsalted
  butter
9 teaspoons double (thick) cream
185 g (6 oz/1 cup) icing sugar, sifted
finely grated peel of 1 orange
3 teaspoons Grand Marnier

Preheat oven to 180C (350F/Gas 4). Butter
several baking sheets. In a bowl, beat butter
with sugar until creamy; beat in egg. Sift
remaining ingredients into bowl, blend in
with spoon, then work by hand to form a soft
dough. Roll out on a floured surface to 0.3 cm
(⅛ in) thick. Using a 5 cm (2 in) fluted
cutter, cut out rounds from dough. Place on
baking sheets; remove centres with a 2 cm (¾
in) cutter. Re-knead and re-roll trimmings:
cut out more rings to make 48 in total.

Bake in the oven for 15 minutes until lightly
browned. Remove to wire racks to cool. Coat
half quantity of rings with melted chocolate;
place on foil. Leave to set. To make filling,
place butter and cream in a bowl; stir over a
saucepan of hot water until butter melts.
Remove from heat. Stir in icing sugar, orange
peel and Grand Marnier. Beat until mixture
cools and thickens. Sandwich plain and
chocolate rings together with cream.

Makes 24.

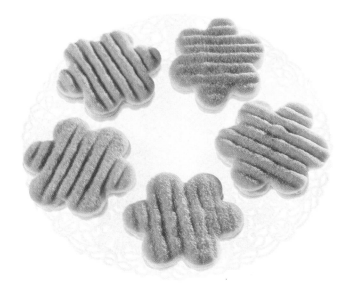

VANILLA CREAMS

BISCUIT DOUGH: 125 g (4 oz/½ cup) butter
60 g (2 oz/¼ cup) caster sugar
1 egg, beaten
few drops vanilla essence
220 g (7 oz/1¾ cups) plain flour
30 g (1 oz/3 tablespoons) cornflour
½ teaspoon baking powder
pinch of salt

VANILLA FILLING: 60 g (2 oz/¼ cup) unsalted
    butter
125 g (4 oz/¾ cup) icing sugar, sifted
1 egg yolk
few drops vanilla essence

TO FINISH: icing sugar for sifting

Preheat oven to 180C (350F/Gas 4). Butter several baking sheets. In a bowl, beat butter with sugar until creamy. Gradually beat in egg, then beat in vanilla to taste. Sift remaining ingredients into bowl and blend in with spoon, then work by hand to form a soft dough. Roll out on a floured surface to 0.3 cm (⅛ in) thick. Mark surface of dough with a ridged rolling pin.

Using a 5 cm (2 in) flower cutter, cut out shapes from dough. Place on baking sheets. Re-knead and re-roll trimmings. Cut out more shapes to make 48 in total. Bake for 15 minutes until very lightly browned. Remove from baking sheets to wire racks to cool. To make filling, in a bowl, beat butter with sugar until creamy. Beat in egg yolk and vanilla to taste. Sandwich biscuits together with mixture. Sift very lightly with icing sugar.

Makes 24.

CHOCOLATE DREAMS

125 g (4 oz/½ cup) butter
60 g (2 oz/¼ cup) caster sugar
1 egg, beaten
220 g (7 oz/1¾ cups) plain flour
30 g (1 oz/¼ cup) cocoa
½ teaspoon baking powder
pinch of salt

GLAZE: 2 teaspoons caster sugar,
   plus a little extra for sprinkling
3 teaspoons milk

CHOCOLATE FILLING: 90 ml (3 fl oz/⅓ cup)
   double (thick) cream
90 g (3 oz) plain (dark) chocolate, chopped

Preheat oven to 180C (350F/Gas 4). Butter
several baking sheets. In a bowl, beat butter
with sugar until creamy; beat in egg. Sift
flour, cocoa, baking powder and salt into
bowl. Blend in with spoon, then work by
hand to form a dough. Roll out on floured
surface, to 0.3 cm (⅛ in) thick. Using 5 cm
(2 in) fancy cutters, cut out shapes from
dough; as desired. Place on baking sheets.
Re-knead and re-roll trimmings. Cut out
more shapes to make 60 in total.

To make glaze, in a small bowl, dissolve sugar
in milk. Brush over biscuits. Bake for 10
minutes. Sprinkle with caster sugar. Cool on
wire racks. To make filling, put cream and
chocolate in a small saucepan. Stir over low
heat until chocolate melts; do not boil. Pour
into a bowl; cool until almost set, then whisk
until fluffy. Sandwich biscuits together with
cream. Leave in a cool place until set.

Makes 30.

— HONEY & LEMON CREAMS —

250 g (8 oz/2 cups) self-raising flour
2 teaspoons bicarbonate of soda
2 teaspoons mixed spice
60 g (2 oz/¼ cup) caster sugar
125 g (4 oz/½ cup) butter
125 g (4 oz/⅓ cup) clear honey

LEMON CREAM: 60 g (2 oz/¼ cup) unsalted
    butter
125 g (4 oz/¾ cup) icing sugar, sifted
finely grated peel of 1 lemon
1 egg yolk
3 teaspoons lemon juice

Preheat oven to 200C (400F/Gas 6). Grease several baking sheets; line with non-stick paper. Sift flour, bicarbonate of soda, spice and sugar into a bowl. Rub in butter until mixture resembles fine breadcrumbs. In a small saucepan, heat honey until melted, but not hot. Pour into flour, then mix to form a dough. Divide dough into 7 g (¼ oz) pieces, about the size of an unshelled hazelnut. Roll each piece into a smooth ball. Place on baking sheets, spaced well apart.

Bake in the oven for 8-10 minutes until golden brown. Allow to cool on baking sheets until firm, then remove to wire racks to cool completely. To make lemon cream, in a bowl, beat butter with sugar and lemon peel until creamy. Beat in egg yolk and lemon juice. Sandwich biscuits together with lemon cream. Leave in a cool place for filling to become firm.

Makes 28.

LIME CREAMS

1 quantity Biscuit Dough, see Vanilla
  Creams page 67

LIME CREAM: 60 g (2 oz/¼ cup) unsalted butter
125 g (4 oz/¾ cup) icing sugar, sifted
very finely grated peel of 1 lime
4 teaspoons lime juice

GLACÉ ICING: 60 g (2 oz/¼ cup) icing sugar,
  sifted
3½ - 4 teaspoons lime juice
few drops of green food colouring

TO FINISH: icing sugar for sifting

Preheat oven to 180C (350F/Gas 4). Butter
several baking sheets. Roll out prepared
biscuit dough, on a floured surface, to 0.3 cm
(⅛ in) thick. Using a 5.5 cm (2¼ in) fluted
cutter, cut out rounds from dough. Place on
baking sheets. Remove centres from half of
rounds with a 4 cm (1½ in) plain round
cutter. Re-knead and re-roll trimmings: cut
out more rounds and rings, making sure you
have an equal number of each to make 44-48
in total. Bake in the oven for 15 minutes until
lightly browned. Remove to wire racks to
cool.

To make lime cream, in a bowl, beat butter
with sugar and lime peel until creamy. Beat in
lime juice. Spread cream onto plain rounds;
place rings on top. Sift icing sugar lightly over
rings. To make glacé icing, in a bowl, blend
sugar with lime juice and a few drops of green
food colouring to make an icing thick enough
to coat back of spoon. Fill centre of rings with
icing. Allow to set.

Makes 22-24.

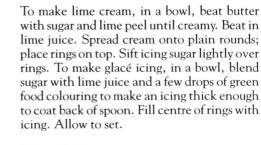

CHESTNUT MERINGUES

2 egg whites
125 g (4 oz/½ cup) caster sugar, plus 2 teaspoons for
  sprinkling
few drops vanilla essence
125 g (4 oz/4) marrons glacé, chopped

TO FINISH: 1 teaspoon sweetened drinking
  chocolate powder

Grease several baking sheets; line with non-stick paper. Preheat oven to 140C (275F/Gas 1). In a very clean, grease-free bowl, whisk egg whites until very stiff, but not dry.

Add about half a tablespoon of sugar; whisk until sugar is incorporated and meringue is stiff and shiny. Continue to add sugar, a little at a time, whisking well between each addition. Whisk in vanilla to taste. Carefully fold in chopped marrons glacé. Using 2 small teaspoons, spoon 36 small oval shapes of mixture onto prepared baking sheets. Lightly sprinkle with the 2 teaspoons caster sugar.

Bake in the oven for 1¼ hours until crisp and dry on outside, yet still soft in centre. Allow to cool. Sift drinking chocolate powder lightly over each meringue. Remove from baking paper.

Makes 36.

Note: These are best eaten freshly made.

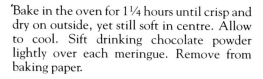

PISTACHIO RINGS

2 egg whites
125 g (4 oz/½ cup) caster sugar
15 g (½ oz/1 tablespoon) pistachio nuts,
   skinned and finely chopped

Grease several baking sheets; line with non-stick paper. Preheat oven to 140C (275F/Gas 1). Put egg whites and sugar into a very clean, grease-free bowl. Place bowl over a saucepan of gently simmering water; whisk until mixture becomes thick and shiny: do not overheat. Remove from heat; continue to whisk until meringue holds stiff peaks.

Spoon meringue into a piping bag fitted with a 1 cm (½ in) 6 point star nozzle. Pipe 36 small rings of meringue on prepared baking sheets, about 5 cm (2 in) in diameter. Sprinkle pistachio nuts over each ring.

Bake in the oven for 1½ hours until dry. Allow to cool. Remove from baking paper.

Makes 36.

Note: Depending on your oven, it may be necessary to select a slightly lower temperature to keep meringues white.

— CHOC & NUT MACAROONS —

rice paper
2 egg whites
185 g (6 oz/¾ cup) caster sugar
185 g (6 oz/1¾ cups) walnuts, finely ground
90 g (3 oz) plain (dark) chocolate, grated
25 walnut halves, cut into halves

Preheat oven to 180C (350F/Gas 4). Line several baking sheets with rice paper. In a very clean, grease-free bowl, whisk egg whites until they hold soft peaks.

Very carefully fold sugar, ground walnuts and chocolate into egg whites until mixture is smooth. Spoon into a piping bag fitted with a 2 cm (¾ in) plain nozzle. Pipe 49-50 small rounds, about 4 cm (1½ in) diameter, on prepared baking sheets, spaced well apart.

Place a walnut quarter in centre of each round. Bake in the oven for 20 minutes. Remove from oven and allow to cool on baking sheets. When cold, remove macaroons from trays and tear away excess rice paper from each one.

Makes 49-50.

— HAZELNUT MACAROONS —

rice paper
2 egg whites
185 g (6 oz/1½ cups) hazelnuts, skinned and
   finely ground
185 g (6 oz/¾ cup) caster sugar
finely grated peel of 1 lemon
½ teaspoon ground cinnamon
10 glacé cherries, cut into quarters

Preheat oven to 180C (350F/Gas 4). Line
several baking sheets with rice paper. In a
very clean, grease-free bowl, whisk egg
whites until they hold soft peaks.

Very carefully fold hazelnuts, sugar, lemon
peel and cinnamon into egg whites until
mixture is smooth. Spoon into a piping bag,
fitted with a 2 cm (¾ in) plain nozzle. Pipe 40
small rounds, about 4 cm (1½ in) diameter,
on prepared baking sheets, spaced well apart.
Place a cherry quarter in centre of each
round.

Bake in the oven for 20 minutes until very
lightly browned. Remove from oven and
allow to cool on baking sheets. When cold,
remove macaroons from sheets and tear away
excess rice paper from each one.

Makes 40.

CAFÉ STERNEN

2 egg whites
125 g (4 oz/½ cup) caster sugar
1 teaspoon coffee essence
28 pecan nuts, or walnuts, cut into halves

TO FINISH: 90 g (3 oz) plain (dark) cake covering
  chocolate, chopped

Preheat oven to 140C (275F/Gas 1). Grease several baking sheets; line with non-stick paper.

In a very clean, grease-free bowl, whisk egg whites until very stiff, but not dry. Add about half a tablespoon of sugar; whisk until incorporated and meringue is stiff and shiny. Continue to add sugar, a little at a time, whisking well between each addition. Whisk in coffee essence. Spoon into a large piping bag fitted with a 2.5 cm (1 in) 12 point star nozzle. Pipe 56 stars onto prepared baking sheets. Press a piece of pecan nut, or walnut, into centre of each star.

Bake in the oven for 1½ hours until dry. Melt chocolate in a double boiler or a small bowl placed over a saucepan of gently simmering water; stir until smooth. Carefully remove meringues from baking paper. Dip base of each one, to a depth of about 0.5 cm (¼ in), in melted chocolate. Pull across the back of a knife to remove excess chocolate. Replace on baking paper until set.

Makes 56.

AMARETTI

1 egg white
2 teaspoons Amaretto di Saronno
155 g (5 oz/1⅓ cups) ground almonds
30 g (1 oz/¼ cup) bitter almonds, blanched
  and finely ground
250 g (8 oz/1½ cups) icing sugar, sifted

TO FINISH: icing sugar for sifting

Preheat oven to 180C (350F/Gas 4). Grease several baking sheets and line with non-stick paper. In a small bowl, very lightly whisk egg white and Amaretto together.

Put ground and bitter almonds and sugar into a large bowl, mix together and make a well in centre. Pour egg white into well, then mix to form a paste.

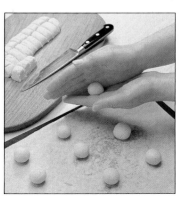

Divide mixture into 36 equal pieces; roll each one into a ball. Place on prepared baking sheets. Bake in the oven for 15-20 minutes until only just lightly browned. Remove from oven; immediately sift evenly with icing sugar. Cool on baking sheets.

Makes 36.

Note: If bitter almonds are unavailable, use 185 g (6 oz/1⅔ cups) ground almonds, adding a few drops of almond essence.

MERINGUE MUSHROOMS

2 egg whites
125 g (4 oz/½ cup) caster sugar
few drops vanilla essence
60 g (2 oz) plain (dark) chocolate, melted

TO FINISH: **1 teaspoon cocoa**

Preheat oven to 140C (275F/Gas 1). Grease
several baking sheets and line with non-stick
paper. In a very clean, grease-free bowl,
whisk egg whites until very stiff, but not dry.
Add about half a tablespoon of sugar: whisk
until incorporated and meringue is stiff and
shiny.

Continue to add sugar, a little at a time,
whisking well between each addition. Whisk
in vanilla to taste. Spoon into a large piping
bag fitted with a 1 cm (½ in) plain nozzle. To
make mushroom caps, pipe 40 rounded
mounds, about 2.5 cm (1 in) in diameter on
baking sheets. To make stalks, pipe 40
pyramid-shaped blobs on baking sheets.

Bake in the oven for 1 hour until dry. Cool on
baking sheets. Remove mushroom caps; cut a
small hole in flat side of each one. Fill with a
little chocolate. Insert pointed ends of stalks
into chocolate. Leave mushrooms upside-
down until chocolate sets. Stand mushrooms
up the right way; sift lightly with cocoa.

Makes 40.

Variations: These may be painted with red
dots, using food colouring, if desired.

MINTY STICKS

2 egg whites
125 g (4 oz/½ cup) caster sugar
1 teaspoon crème de menthe
60 g (2 oz) crisp mint-flavoured chocolate
   sticks, finely chopped
2 teaspoons chocolate sprinkles

Preheat oven to 140C (275F/Gas 1). Grease several baking sheets and line with non-stick paper.

In a very clean, grease-free bowl, whisk egg whites until very stiff, but not dry. Add about half a tablespoon of sugar; whisk until incorporated and meringue is stiff and shiny. Continue to add sugar, a little at a time, whisking well between each addition. Whisk in crème de menthe, then fold in chocolate sticks.

Spoon meringue into a large piping bag fitted with a 1 cm (½ in) plain nozzle. Pipe 56 lengths of meringue, 7.5 cm (3 in) long, onto prepared baking sheets. Sprinkle with chocolate sprinkles. Bake in the oven for 1 hour until dry. Allow to cool on baking sheets, then carefully remove from paper.

Makes 56.

JAPONAIS SANDWICHES

2 egg whites
125 g (4 oz/½ cup) caster sugar
60 g (2 oz/½ cup) hazelnuts, skinned,
  toasted and finely ground

FILLING: 30 g (1 oz/6 teaspoons) unsalted
  butter
45 g (1½ oz/3 tablespoons) icing sugar, sifted
1 egg yolk
30 g (1 oz/¼ cup) hazelnuts, skinned,
  toasted and finely ground

TO FINISH: icing sugar for sifting

Cut sheets of non-stick paper to fit several baking sheets. Draw 42 circles, 5 cm (2 in) in diameter, on the paper. Grease baking sheets and place paper, drawn circles side down, on baking sheets. Preheat oven to 140C (275F/Gas 1). In a very clean, grease-free bowl, whisk egg whites until very stiff, but not dry. Add about half a tablespoon of sugar; whisk until incorporated and meringue is stiff and shiny. Continue to add sugar, a little at a time, whisking well between each addition.

Fold hazelnuts into meringue. Spoon into piping bag, fitted with a 10 mm (⅜ in) plain nozzle. Following drawn circles, pipe spirals of meringue onto baking sheets. Bake in the oven for 1¼ hours until dry. Cool on baking sheets. To make filling, beat butter with sugar in a bowl until creamy. Beat in egg yolk and hazelnuts. Remove meringues from paper; sandwich together with hazelnut cream. Sift with icing sugar.

Makes 21.

VALENTINE HEART

60 g (2 oz/¼ cup) butter
30 g (1 oz/5 teaspoons) caster sugar
2 egg yolks
few drops vanilla essence
100 g (3½ oz/¾ cup) plain flour
15 g (½ oz/6 teaspoons) cornflour
½ teaspoon baking powder

ICING: 2 egg whites
375 g (12 oz/2¼ cups) icing sugar, sifted
few drops pink food colouring

TO DECORATE: 1 pink rose and 1 white rose,
1 egg white, very lightly beaten
60 g (2 oz/¼ cup) caster sugar

To prepare decoration, gently remove petals from roses. Very lightly brush petals with egg white and coat lightly with caster sugar. Shake off excess sugar. Place rose petals on greaseproof paper. Leave to dry for about 1 hour.

Preheat oven to 180C (350F/Gas 4). Butter a large baking sheet. In a bowl, beat butter with sugar until creamy. Beat in egg yolks and vanilla to taste. Sift flour, cornflour and baking powder into bowl. Blend in with a spoon, then work by hand to form a soft dough. Knead lightly on a floured surface until smooth. Roll out to an oblong, about 27.5 x 22.5 (11 x 9 in). Place on baking sheet.

Using a paper or cardboard template, cut out a large heart from dough. Remove trimmings and use these to make small biscuits. Bake heart in the oven for 20 minutes until very lightly browned . Remove from baking sheet to a wire rack to cool.

When heart is cold, place wire rack on a baking sheet. To make icing, mix egg whites in a bowl with 280 g (9 oz/1 cup, plus 2 tablespoons) of icing sugar, to make an icing thick enough to coat the back of a spoon evenly. Colour it a delicate pink with a few drops of food colouring. Pour icing onto heart and spread out with a palette knife to coat evenly. Leave on rack until icing is almost set. Spoon excess icing on baking sheet into a bowl; cover surface with plastic wrap. Set aside.

Just before icing on heart is completely set, decorate with prepared rose petals; pressing them gently into icing to secure. Beat remaining icing sugar into reserved icing. Spoon into a piping bag fitted with a small plain writing nozzle. Pipe your own valentine message on heart, if desired. Pipe a decorative border around edge of heart. Leave to set.

Makes 1.

— TRADITIONAL SHORTBREAD —

125 g (4 oz/½ cup) butter
30 g (1 oz/5 teaspoons) caster sugar
155 g (5 oz/1¼ cups) plain flour
pinch of salt
30 g (1 oz/2 tablespoons) fine semolina

TO FINISH: caster sugar for sprinkling

In a bowl, beat butter with sugar until creamy. Sift flour and salt into bowl, then add semolina. Blend in with a spoon, then work by hand to form a soft dough.

Knead dough lightly on a floured surface until smooth. Roll out to a smooth round, about 15 cm (6 in) in diameter. Very lightly flour a 17.5 cm (7 in) shortbread mould. Place shortbread, smooth-side down, in mould. Press out to fit mould exactly. Very carefully unmould shortbread onto a baking sheet. Refrigerate for 1 hour. (If you do not have a shortbread mould, shape dough into a neat round. Place on baking sheet, prick well with a fork, then pinch edge to decorate.)

Preheat oven to 160C (325F/Gas 3). Bake shortbread in the oven for 35-40 minutes until cooked through. Shortbread should remain pale in colour. Immediately shortbread is removed from oven, sprinkle very lightly with caster sugar. Allow to cool on baking sheet for about 20 minutes, then very carefully remove to a wire rack to cool completely.

Makes 1.

— CHRISTMAS SHORTBREAD —

220 g (7 oz/1¾ cups) plain flour
pinch of salt
30 g (1 oz/3 tablespoons) cornflour
60 g (2 oz/¼ cup) caster sugar
250 g (8 oz/1 cup) butter

TO DECORATE: about 37 blanched almonds
about 19 walnut halves
7 green glacé cherries, cut into halves
5 red glacé cherries, cut into halves

TO FINISH: caster sugar for sprinkling

Sift flour, salt and cornflour into a bowl, then add sugar.

Rub butter into flour until mixture forms coarse crumbs. Gently work mixture together to form a soft dough. Roll out dough, on a floured surface, to a round a little smaller than a 25 cm (10 in) loose-bottomed fluted flan tin. Place dough in tin and press out gently to fit tin exactly, pressing well into flutes. Smooth surface with the back of a spoon. Prick well with a fork.

To decorate shortbread, arrange almonds in a neat ring around edge of dough. Add a ring of walnut halves; a ring of green cherries, then a ring of red cherries. Place a walnut half in centre. Refrigerate shortbread for 30 minutes. Preheat oven to 180C (350F/Gas 4). Bake shortbread in the oven for 45-50 minutes until lightly browned. Cool in tin. Sift lightly with caster sugar. Carefully remove from tin onto a serving plate.

Serves 16.

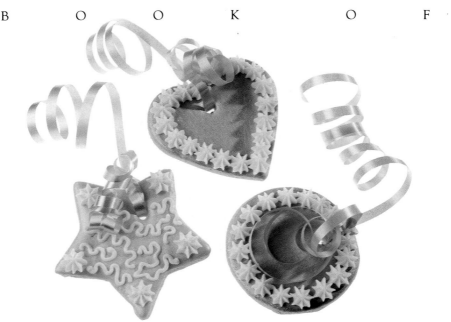

CHRISTMAS TREE COOKIES

155 g (5 oz/⅔ cup) butter
90 g (3 oz/⅓ cup) caster sugar
3 egg yolks
2 teaspoons orange flower water
250 g (8 oz/2 cups) plain flour
1 teaspoon baking powder

TO DECORATE: 2 egg whites
500 g (1 lb/3 cups) icing sugar, sifted
edible gold and silver lustre powders
thin ribbon of various colours

Preheat oven to 180C (350F/Gas 4). Butter
several baking sheets.

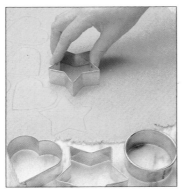

In a bowl, beat butter with sugar until
creamy. Beat in egg yolks and orange flower
water. Sift flour and baking powder into bowl;
blend in with a spoon, then work by hand to
form a soft dough. Knead lightly, on a floured
surface, until smooth. Roll out to 0.3 cm (⅛
in) thick. Using 6 cm (2½ in) shaped cutters,
cut out rounds, stars and hearts from dough.
Place on baking sheets. Re-knead and re-roll
trimmings and cut out more shapes.
Continue until dough is used up to make 28
in total.

Using a skewer, make a small hole in each
shape about 1 cm (½ in) in from top edge.
Ensure hole is large enough to thread ribbon
through. Bake in the oven for 15-18 minutes
until very lightly browned. Remove from
baking sheets to wire racks to cool.

To decorate biscuits, mix egg whites in a bowl with two-thirds of icing sugar, to make an icing thick enough to coat the back of a spoon. Brush icing thinly and evenly over each biscuit. Allow to dry. Meanwhile, beat remaining icing sugar into remaining icing, beating until icing holds stiff peaks. Cover with plastic wrap to prevent drying.

On 2 small saucers, blend gold and silver lustre powders with water to make smooth thin pastes. Paint biscuits with lustres. Allow to dry for about 1 hour.

Decorate shapes with reserved icing simply by applying in small flecks, or more decoratively by piping. Allow to dry. Thread biscuits onto coloured ribbons and hang on Christmas tree. If biscuits are left on tree for too long they will dry out, so keep a supply in an airtight tin to replenish tree.

Makes 28.

EASTER BISCUITS

185 g (6 oz/¾ cup) butter
185 g (6 oz/¾ cup) caster sugar
3 egg yolks
4 teaspoons orange flower water
6 teaspoons milk
125 g (4 oz/¾ cup) currants
500 g (1 lb/4 cups) plain flour
pinch of salt

GLAZE: 1 egg white, very lightly beaten
6 teaspoons caster sugar

Preheat oven to 180C (350F/Gas 4). Butter several baking sheets. In a bowl, beat butter with sugar until creamy. Beat in egg yolks, orange flower water and milk.

Add currants. Sift flour and salt into bowl and mix in to form a fairly stiff dough. Knead lightly, on a floured surface, until smooth. Roll out to 0.3 cm (⅛ in) thick. Using a 6 cm (2½ in) round fluted cutter, cut out rounds from dough. Place on baking sheets. Re-knead and re-roll trimmings: cut out more rounds. Continue until dough is used to make 54-56 in total.

Bake in the oven for 10 minutes, then remove from oven. Brush with egg white and sift lightly with caster sugar. Return to oven for a further 5-10 minutes until lightly browned. Remove from baking sheets to wire racks to cool.

Makes 54-56.

EASTER BUNNIES

125 g (4 oz/½ cup) butter
125 g (4 oz/½ cup) caster sugar
1 egg, beaten
few drops vanilla essence
60 g (2 oz/⅔ cup) desiccated coconut
250 g (8 oz/2 cups) plain flour
pinch of salt
½ teaspoon baking powder

TO FINISH: icing sugar for sifting, if desired

Preheat oven to 180C (350F/Gas 4). Butter several baking sheets. In a bowl, beat butter with sugar until creamy. Beat in egg and vanilla to taste.

Stir in coconut. Sift flour, salt and baking powder into creamed mixture. Blend in with a spoon, then work by hand to form a soft dough. Knead lightly, on a floured surface, until smooth. Roll out to 0.3 cm (⅛ in) thick. Using a rabbit-shaped cutter, cut out shapes from dough. Place on baking sheets. Re-knead and re-roll trimmings: cut out more shapes. Continue until dough is used up to make up to 60 in total, depending on size of cutter.

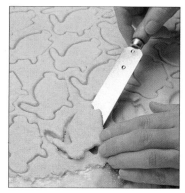

Bake in the oven for 15 minutes until very lightly browned. Remove from baking sheets to wire racks to cool. When cold, sift lightly with icing sugar, if desired.

Makes about 60.

ADVENT CRESCENTS

250 g (8 oz/2 cups) plain flour
pinch of salt
125 g (4 oz/½ cup) caster sugar
155 g (5 oz/1⅓ cups) ground almonds
250 g (8 oz/1 cup) butter, cut into small cubes
3 egg yolks
few drops almond essence

TO FINISH: **icing sugar for sifting**

Sift flour and salt into a bowl; mix in sugar and ground almonds. Make a well in centre.

Place butter, egg yolks and almond essence in centre of mixture. With fingertips, gently work butter with egg yolks, gradually incorporating flour, sugar and almonds until mixture forms a soft dough. Wrap in plastic wrap and refrigerate for 30 minutes. Preheat oven to 180C (350F/Gas 4).

Divide dough into 15 g (½ oz) pieces, about the size of a walnut. Shape each piece into a thin roll, about 10 cm (4 in) long. Curve round to form a crescent shape. Place on ungreased baking sheets. Bake in the oven for 15 minutes until lightly browned. Allow to cool on baking sheets. Sift liberally with icing sugar. Remove from baking sheets to a serving plate.

Makes 42.

LEBKUCHEN

SPICED HONEY DOUGH: 375 g (12 oz/3 cups) self-raising
   flour
2 teaspoons mixed spice
pinch of salt
90 g (3 oz/¼ cup) clear honey
185 g (6 oz/1 cup) dark soft brown sugar
45 g (1½ oz/9 teaspoons) butter
1 egg, beaten
finely grated peel of 1 lemon
1 tablespoon lemon juice

TO DECORATE: 250 g (8 oz) plain (dark) cake covering
   chocolate, melted
1 egg white
250 g (8 oz/1½ cups) icing sugar, sifted
edible silver balls

Preheat oven to 180C (350F/Gas 4). Butter a
large baking sheet. Sift flour, spice and salt
into a bowl, then make a well in centre. Put
honey, sugar and butter into a saucepan and
stir over low heat until melted. Cool slightly.
Pour into flour; add egg, lemon peel and
juice. Mix to form a soft dough. Knead on a
floured surface until smooth. Roll out to an
oblong, about 27.5 x 22.5 cm (11 x 9 in).
Place on baking sheet. Using a paper or
cardboard template, cut out a large heart
shape.

Remove trimmings from around heart and
use to make gingerbread men. Bake heart in
the oven for 20-25 minutes until lightly
browned. If necessary trim to shape while still
warm. Remove to wire rack to cool. When
cold, place rack on a large baking sheet and
coat heart with melted chocolate. Allow to
set. In a bowl, beat egg white with icing sugar
until mixture holds stiff peaks. Decorate
heart, simply or elaborately, with icing and
silver balls.

Makes 1.

GINGERBREAD HOUSE

2 quantities Spiced Honey Dough,
see Lebkuchen page 93

ROYAL ICING: 4 egg whites
1 kg (2 lb/6 cups) icing sugar, sifted
2 teaspoons lemon juice
2 teaspoons glycerine

TO DECORATE: 1 packet clear fruit drops
20 long, thin, crisp chocolate mint sticks
1 packet fruit jellies
1 packet candy-coated chocolate drops
22 walnut halves
14 blanched almonds
2 small chocolate flake bars

Preheat oven to 180C (350F/Gas 4). Butter
three 32.5 x 22.5 cm (13 x 9 in) Swiss roll
tins. (If you only have one tin, bake one tin at
a time.) Divide dough into 3 equal pieces.
Roll out each piece, on a well floured surface,
to an oblong large enough to fit prepared tins.
Trim edges; place in tins. Bake in the oven for
20-25 minutes until lightly browned. To be
able to cut cooked dough into shapes without
hurrying, stagger baking times by placing tins
in oven at 10 minute intervals.

MUESLI COOKIES

185 g (6 oz/¾ cup) butter
90 g (3 oz/⅓ cup) caster sugar
90 g (3 oz/¼ cup) clear honey
finely grated peel of 1 orange
1 egg
60 g (2 oz/½ cup) self-raising flour
pinch of salt
375 g (12 oz/3 cups) muesli

Preheat oven to 180C (350F/Gas 4). Butter several baking sheets. In a bowl, beat butter with caster sugar until creamy. Beat in honey, orange peel and egg. Sift flour and salt into bowl and blend in with a spoon.

Add muesli to creamed mixture, then work in by hand to form a soft dough. Roll out on a floured surface to 0.5 cm (¼ in) thick. Using a 6 cm (2½ in) plain round cutter, cut rounds from dough. Place on baking sheets. Re-knead and re-roll trimmings: cut out more rounds. Continue until dough is used up to make 29-30 in total.

Bake in the oven for 20-25 minutes until very lightly browned. Allow to cool on baking sheets for a few minutes, then remove to wire racks to cool completely.

Makes 29-30.

HONEY DOUBLES

60 g (2 oz/½ cup) self-raising flour
1 teaspoon bicarbonate of soda
60 g (2 oz/⅓ cup) dark soft brown sugar
185 g (6 oz/2 cups) rolled oats
90 g (3 oz/⅓ cup) butter
90 g (3 oz/¼ cup) clear honey, melted and
   cooled

FILLING: 60 g (2 oz/¼ cup) unsalted butter
90 g (3 oz/½ cup) icing sugar, sifted
1 tablespoon clear honey
2 teaspoons lemon juice

Preheat oven to 180C (350F/Gas 4). Butter
several baking sheets.

Sift flour, bicarbonate of soda and sugar into a
bowl, then mix in oats. Rub in butter until
mixture resembles coarse breadcrumbs. Add
honey; mix to form a soft dough. Roll out on a
floured surface to 0.3 cm (⅛ in) thick. Using
a 5 cm (2 in) plain round cutter, cut out
rounds from dough. Place on baking sheets.
Re-knead and re-roll trimmings: cut out
rounds. Continue until dough is used up to
make 32 in total. Bake in the oven for 15-20
minutes until lightly browned. Cool on wire
racks.

To make filling, in a bowl, beat butter with
sugar until creamy. Beat in honey and lemon
juice. Refrigerate for about 10 minutes to firm
up. Sandwich biscuits together with honey
cream. Keep cool to prevent filling from
softening.

Makes 16.

WHEAT BRAN BISCUITS

125 g (4 oz/2 cups) wheat bran breakfast cereal
90 g (3 oz/⅓ cup) demerara sugar
125 g (4 oz/1 cup) self-raising flour
90 g (3 oz/⅓ cup) butter
60 g (2 oz/⅓ cup) currants
1 egg, beaten
milk for glazing

TO FINISH: caster sugar for sprinkling

Preheat oven to 180C (350F/Gas 4). Butter several baking sheets. Put cereal into a food processor and process for about 30 seconds until finely ground.

Add sugar and flour to processor and process for a few seconds to blend with cereal. Add butter and process for a few seconds until mixture resembles coarse breadcrumbs. Add currants and egg; process until mixture forms a soft dough. Roll out dough on a floured surface to 0.3 cm (⅛ in) thick. Using a 6 cm (2½ in) fluted round cutter, cut out rounds. Place on baking sheets. Re-knead and re-roll trimmings: cut out more rounds to make 32-34 in total.

Brush each biscuit with a little milk to glaze. Bake in the oven for 20-25 minutes until lightly browned. Remove from oven and immediately sprinkle with caster sugar. Allow to cool on baking sheets for a few minutes, then remove to wire racks to cool completely.

Makes 32-34.

PEANUT & RAISIN BARS

185 g (6 oz/¾ cup) butter
60 g (2 oz/¼ cup) demerara sugar
125 g (4 oz/⅓ cup) clear honey
125 g (4 oz/¾ cup) mixed peanuts and raisins,
    coarsely chopped
250 g (8 oz/2¾ cups) rolled oats

Preheat oven to 200C (400F/Gas 6). Butter a 32.5 x 22.5 cm (13 x 9 in) Swiss roll tin. Put butter, sugar and honey into a large saucepan; stir over a low heat until melted and sugar is dissolved.

Stir in peanuts, raisins and oats. Spread mixture evenly in prepared tin. Bake in the oven for 20 minutes until golden brown, then mark into bars: cutting evenly into 3 lengthwise, then 10 widthwise. Leave in tin until completely cold.

To remove from baking tin, re-cut through marked lines and remove bars with a small flexible palette knife.

Makes 30.

Variation: Instead of peanuts and raisins, use walnuts, almonds, or hazelnuts, mixed with raisins. Or use all nuts, or all raisins, if desired.

RAISIN OAT BISCUITS

185 g (6 oz/1⅓ cups) wholemeal flour
60 g (2 oz/½ cup) fine oatmeal
60 g (2 oz/¼ cup) demerara sugar
pinch of salt
1 teaspoon baking powder
125 g (4 oz/½ cup) butter
60 g (2 oz/⅓ cup) raisins
1 egg, beaten

Preheat oven to 190C (375F/Gas 5). Butter several baking sheets. Put flour, oatmeal, sugar, salt and baking powder into a bowl; mix well.

Rub butter into flour and oatmeal until mixture resembles fine breadcrumbs. Mix in raisins. Add egg and mix to form a soft dough. Roll out on a floured surface to 0.3 cm (⅛ in) thick. Using a 6 cm (2½ in) plain round cutter, cut out rounds from dough. Place on baking sheets. Re-knead and re-roll trimmings: cut out more rounds. Continue until dough is used up to make 22 in total.

Bake in the oven for 15-20 minutes until lightly browned. Allow to cool on baking sheets for a few minutes, then remove to wire racks to cool completely.

Makes 22.

Variation: Raisins may be omitted, if desired.

— SESAME SEED CRACKERS —

250 g (8 oz/1¾ cups) wholemeal flour
½ teaspoon salt
½ teaspoon baking powder
90 g (3 oz/⅓ cup) butter
1 egg, beaten
6 teaspoons milk, plus a little extra for glazing
30 g (1 oz/¼ cup) sesame seeds

Preheat oven to 180C (350F/Gas 4). Butter several baking sheets. Put flour, salt and baking powder into a bowl and mix well.

Rub butter into flour until mixture resembles fine breadcrumbs. Add egg and milk and mix to form a stiff dough. Roll out on a floured surface to 0.3 cm (⅛ in) thick. Using a 6 cm (2½ in) plain round cutter, cut out rounds from dough. Place on baking sheets. Re-knead and re-roll trimmings: cut out more rounds. Continue until dough is used up to make 20 in total.

Brush biscuits with a little milk to glaze, then sprinkle evenly with sesame seeds. Bake in the oven for 15-20 minutes until lightly browned. Remove to wire racks to cool. Serve with cheese or pâté.

Makes 20.

SCOTTISH OATCAKES

125 g (4 oz/1 cup) fine oatmeal
½ teaspoon baking powder
pinch of salt
30 g (1 oz/6 teaspoons) butter
6 teaspoons boiling water

Put oatmeal, baking powder and salt into a bowl, then rub in butter until mixture resembles coarse breadcrumbs. Add boiling water, mix to form a dough and knead until smooth. Dough will be sticky at first, but when kneaded will become drier and smoother as oatmeal absorbs water.

Roll out dough on a surface sprinkled with oatmeal to a round a little larger than 20 cm (8 in). Using a plate as a guide, cut dough into a neat round. Cut round into 8 equal pieces to form neat triangles.

Heat a griddle over a moderate heat and grease very lightly. Place oatcakes on griddle and cook for 8-10 minutes until well cooked through and corners curl upwards. Cool on a wire rack. Serve with butter and marmalade.

Makes 8.

— CHEESE STRAWS OR PLAITS —

125 g (4 oz/1 cup) plain flour
½ teaspoon baking powder
pinch of salt
good pinch of cayenne pepper
¼ teaspoon dry mustard
105 g (3½ oz/¾ cup) grated Parmesan cheese
90 g (3 oz/⅓ cup) butter
3 egg yolks
2 teaspoons water
1 egg white, very lightly beaten

TO FINISH: paprika for sprinkling

Preheat oven to 200C (400F/Gas 6). Butter several baking sheets.

Sift flour, baking powder, salt, pepper and mustard into a bowl, then mix in all but 3 teaspoons of Parmesan. Rub in butter until mixture resembles fine breadcrumbs. Add egg yolks and water and mix to form a dough. Roll out on a floured surface to an oblong about 32.5 x 22.5 cm (13 x 9 in). Trim edges. Brush with egg white and sprinkle evenly with remaining Parmesan. To make straws, cut in half lengthwise. To make plaits; cut in half widthwise.

For straws; cut across each strip into thin straws, a little under 0.5 cm (¼ in) wide. For plaits; cut into long thin strips: plait together in pairs. Place on baking sheets. Re-knead and re-roll trimmings. Using 6 cm (2½ in) and 4.5 cm (1¾ in) plain round cutters, cut out 10 rings. Place on baking sheets. Bake for 8-10 minutes until only lightly browned. Cool on wire racks. Sprinkle with paprika. Fill rings with straws.

Makes 100.

SESAME STICKS

185 g (6 oz/1½ cups) plain flour
½ teaspoon baking powder
½ teaspoon salt
90 g (3 oz/⅓ cup) butter
60 ml (2 fl oz/¼ cup) boiling water
1 small egg, beaten
60 g (2 oz/½ cup) sesame seeds

Preheat oven to 180C (350F/Gas 4). Butter several baking sheets. Sift flour, baking powder and salt into a bowl. Rub in butter until mixture resembles fine breadcrumbs. Add boiling water and mix to form a soft dough.

Knead dough lightly on a floured surface until smooth. Divide into 18 equal pieces, about 15 g (½ oz) each. Roll each piece of dough into a long thin strand, about 30-35 cm (12-14 in) long. Place on baking sheets. Brush strands with egg.

Sprinkle evenly with sesame seeds. Bake in the oven for 20 minutes until lightly browned. Very carefully remove from baking sheets to wire racks to cool. Serve with cocktails or pre-dinner drinks.

Makes 18.

CARAWAY PRETZELS

185 g (6 oz/1½ cups) plain flour
½ teaspoon baking powder
½ teaspoon salt
90 g (3 oz/⅓ cup) butter
3 teaspoons caraway seeds
60 ml (2 fl oz/¼ cup) boiling water
1 egg white, very lightly beaten

Preheat oven to 180C (350F/Gas 4). Butter several baking sheets. Sift flour, baking powder and salt into a bowl. Rub in butter until mixture resembles fine breadcrumbs, then mix in 1 teaspoon of caraway seeds. Add boiling water and mix to form a soft dough.

Knead dough lightly on a floured surface until smooth. Divide into 36 equal pieces, about 7 g (¼ oz) each. Take one piece of dough and shape into a long thin strand, about 35 cm (14 in) long. Bring ends round to form a loop; cross over, then take back up to top of loop. Press firmly in position to secure. Place on a baking sheet. Repeat with remaining pieces of dough.

Brush pretzels with egg white and sprinkle evenly with remaining caraway seeds. Bake in the oven for 18-20 minutes until lightly browned. Carefully remove from baking sheets to wire racks to cool.

Makes 36.

ONION & GARLIC TWISTS

90 g (3 oz/⅓ cup) butter
2 cloves garlic, crushed
2 teaspoons very finely grated onion
3 egg yolks
2 teaspoons water
185 g (6 oz/1½ cups) plain flour
½ teaspoon baking powder
¼ teaspoon salt
1 egg white, very lightly beaten
coarse salt for sprinkling

Preheat oven to 200C (400F/Gas 6). Butter several baking sheets. In a bowl, beat butter until creamy.

Beat in garlic, onion, egg yolks and water. Sift flour, baking powder and salt into bowl. Blend in with a spoon, then work by hand to form a soft dough. Knead lightly on a floured surface until smooth. Roll out to an oblong, about 35 x 25 cm (14 x 10 in). Trim edges. Cut in half widthwise. Using a pastry wheel, or a knife, cut dough into 32-36 thin strips, measuring about 17.5 x 0.5 cm (7 x ¼ in).

Taking one strip at a time, carefully twist strips and place on baking sheets. Brush with egg white and sprinkle lightly with coarse salt. Bake in the oven for 15 minutes until lightly browned. Very carefully remove from baking sheets to wire racks to cool.

Makes 32-36.

CHEESE & HERB BISCUITS

125 g (4 oz/1 cup) plain flour
½ teaspoon baking powder
¼ teaspoon salt
90 g (3 oz/⅓ cup) butter
90 g (3 oz/¾ cup) grated Cheddar cheese
3 egg yolks
2 teaspoons water

FILLING: 45 g (1½ oz/9 teaspoons) butter
1 teaspoon snipped fresh chives
½ teaspoon dried mixed herbs
45 g (1½ oz/⅓ cup) grated Cheddar cheese
salt and pepper

TO FINISH: paprika for sprinkling

Preheat oven to 200C (400F/Gas 6). Butter several baking sheets. Sift flour, baking powder and salt into a bowl. Rub in butter until mixture resembles fine breadcrumbs; mix in cheese. Add egg yolks and water; mix to form a dough. Knead lightly on a floured surface until smooth. Roll out thinly . Prick all over with a fork. Using a 5 cm (2 in) plain round cutter, cut out rounds from dough. Place on baking sheets. Re-knead and re-roll trimmings: cut out more rounds to make 60 in total.

Bake in the oven for 10-15 minutes until lightly browned. Remove to wire racks to cool. To make filling, in a bowl, beat butter with herbs until creamy. Beat in cheese. Season well with salt and pepper. Sandwich biscuits together with herb butter. Sprinkle lightly with paprika. Serve chilled.

Makes 30.

CURRY BISCUITS

185 g (6 oz/1½ cups) plain flour
½ teaspoon baking powder
¼ teaspoon salt
2 teaspoons medium-hot curry powder
90 g (3 oz/⅓ cup) butter
1 egg
1 teaspoon tomato purée (paste)

Preheat oven to 200C (400F/Gas 6). Butter several baking sheets. Sift flour, baking powder, salt and curry powder into a bowl. Rub in butter until mixture resembles fine breadcrumbs. Make a well in centre.

In a small bowl, whisk egg and tomato purée together, then pour into well in centre of flour. Mix to form a soft dough. Knead lightly on a floured surface until smooth. Roll out to 0.3 cm (⅛ in) thick. Using a biscuit wheel, or a knife, cut dough into oblongs about 7.5 x 4.5 cm (3 x 1¾ in). Place on baking sheets. Re-knead and re-roll trimmings: cut out more biscuits. Continue until dough is used up to make 28-30 in total.

Bake in the oven for 12-15 minutes until very lightly browned. Remove from baking sheets to wire racks to cool. Serve with cheese or with savoury dips.

Makes 28-30

Clockwise from top:

Spiced Oat Cookies, page 98

Easter Biscuits, page 90

Peanut & Raisin Bars, page 102

Wheat Bran Biscuits, page 101

Advent Crescents, page 92

Almond Flowers, page 46

Muesli Cookies, page 99

Hazelnut Macaroons, page 78

Clockwise from top:

Fine Scroll Biscuits, page 59

Triple Orange Drops, page 60

Shrewsbury Biscuits, page 41

Viennese Fingers, page 56

Chocolate Pretzels, page 48

Pinwheels, page 47

Cherry Praline Rings, page 40

Clockwise from top:

Pistachio Rings, page 76

Chocolate Dreams, page 68

Café Sternen, page 79

Choc & Nut Macaroons, page 77

Orange & Chocolate Rings, page 66

Spiced Spritz Cookies, page 64

Clockwise from top:

Cheese Plaits, page 106

Curry Biscuits, page 115

Sesame Seed Crackers, page 104

Water Biscuits, page 108

INDEX